The
Reign
of the
Vedic Gods

The
Reign
of the
Vedic Gods

The Galaxy of Hindu Gods
Book 1

SWAMI ACHUTHANANDA

The author can be contacted at *swamia@mmmgh.com*

Editor: Polly Kummel, *www.amazinphrasin.com*
Page Layout and Design: *wordzworth.com*
Cover Design: Cathi Stevenson, *www.BookCoverExpress.com*
Photo Credit: *www.depositphotos.com* and public domain (Wikimedia Commons)

ISBN: 978-0-9757883-1-8

Relianz Communications Pty Ltd,
Queensland 4035, Australia.
Email: *contact@relianz.com.au*

Dedicated to my wife,
for the idea and inspiration.

Contents

Dear Reader,

Some time ago I published a book entitled *Many Many Many Gods of Hinduism*, which was a shortcut to learning Hinduism. Shortly after the book's publication, I received emails from around the world. People from Sydney to Boston wrote to say how the book had enhanced their appreciation of the religion. Many also expressed their interest in knowing more about Indian mythology. This book was born as a result but only after a gestation period of several years. While *Many Many Many Gods of Hinduism* helped them understand the essence of the religion, the scenic path of mythology—teeming with gods and goddesses and their stories—can be daunting to the uninitiated.

Why, you may ask? India has one of the longest recorded mythologies in world history. It is also one of the rare places where folktales still constitute a key part of the living culture. Although these tales were stretched and twisted and molded over the years, India never abandoned its gods. As Jawaharlal Nehru, the former prime minister of India, put it, "India does not abolish the bullock cart when the Boeing jet arrives."

You will be surprised to learn that Hindu gods and goddesses are not paragons of perfection. In fact the notion of god is often challenged. Krishna spent his childhood as a world-famous butter thief and his adolescence as a romantic lover before he became a spiritual advisor who dispensed timeless wisdom. If you are a puritan, the deeds of Shiva will embarrass you to no end, just as his feats will inspire you and leave you in awe. You will find many unsavory characters, some with extensive criminal histories. Polygamy was rampant in those times, and deceit and treachery were the order of the day. But that's only when you view a 5000-year-old mythology from a 21st century vantage point. The gods and goddesses are perfect only in their spheres of activity. Outside their spheres they make mistakes just like you and me, and are punished, leading them to change their behavior and correct their ways.

Let us travel back in time to meet these heroes and read of their deeds that have been transformed into mythical figures and stories. These stories have everything—romance, magic, action, *maithuna* (sex), weirdness, and unforgettable characters. Yet these are not merely tales of courage and bravery but lessons about our culture, heritage, and history. For Indians truth is timeless and unchanging. It doesn't matter how it is expressed or whether it was created today or a thousand years ago. "Truth alone triumphs" is the national motto of India. While reading these stories if you experience an epiphany, rest assured that you are not alone. Many of the greatest contributions to Indian culture—from the sexually explicit reliefs of Khajuraho to Bollywood dancing—have drawn inspiration from Indian mythology.

Swami Achuthananda (Sach)

P.S. My goal was to write everything about Hindu deities in a single book and make it comprehensive enough that the reader would have no need to consult other texts. But after I wrote the last chapter, I realized the contents will not fit into a decent-sized book without the reader enduring elbow pain for print versions and scroll blur for e-versions. I strongly suspect that the thicker the book, the less it's lifted up and read. To resolve this dilemma I consulted the mythological Hindu gods for inspiration. Ancient Hindu gods are known for their highly creative problem-solving skills. The architect-cum-engineer Vishwakarma shaved off the brightness of Surya with his heavenly lathe so that the sun god's wife could live with him happily ever after. On another occasion Vishnu chopped the dead body of Sati into many pieces with his discus to relieve the mourning Shiva of grief. Taking a cue from mythology, I decided to chop the book into many parts, so that each part would be light enough to not inflict any major damage to the human skeletal system.

Now, don't worry if you haven't heard of Vishwakarma or Surya. We'll come across them on our journey, even in this, the first volume of a multivolume collection about Hindu deities and their timeless tales.

1

Ganesha – The Obstacle Remover

If you find a path with no obstacles,
it probably doesn't lead anywhere.

—FRANK A. CLARK, 1860-1936

What? An elephant-headed god?" This is the typical reaction of those unfamiliar with India's favorite deity, but anyone from the subcontinent, regardless of age, class, creed, religion, or gender, will immediately recognize Ganesha with his prominent pot belly, large ears, and trunk for sampling delicacies. Welcome to the galaxy of Hindu gods where, in addition to the elephant-faced Ganesha, you will occasionally come across boar-faced, bear-faced, horse-faced, lion-faced, or even monkey-faced gods. With an elephant's head and the body of a man, Ganesha always fails the personality test, yet he is one of the most beloved deities of the pantheon. In fact a great Indian tradition is to start every venture with the blessings of Ganesha, the ultimate obstacle remover. That is why

Ganesha is first on our journey to meet the Hindu gods even though, strictly speaking, he has no place in a book about Vedic gods.

Ganesha—India's most popular deity

Despite his strange looks, Ganesha comes from an illustrious family. Those who are familiar with India know the country is famous for its dynasties. The Kapoor family dominates Bollywood, the Tatas reign in business, and the Gandhi clan is preeminent in politics. A long-standing member of the Shaiva dynasty, Ganesha is the son of Shiva, the fearless leader of the Shaivites, which have a following of more than 300 million devotees. Ganesha's mother is Parvati, who is regarded as supreme by the equally strong Shakta sect. And he has a sibling named Kartikeya, who, as Muruga, is well known among the Tamil community, not only in India but also in Singapore, Malaysia, and other countries. Although Ganesha is generally considered the older brother of Kartikeya, there are lingering doubts about who is older.[1] When it comes to popularity, however, there's no doubt. Born to a family of spiritual heavyweights, Ganesha beats them all in popularity, for his fame has spread to religions like Buddhism and Jainism. With a worldwide following rivaling that of Santa Claus, Ganesha has become a deity attached to no specific religion, although his origins are undoubtedly rooted in Hinduism.

Ganesha relaxing at Wat Saman Rattanaram Temple in Chachoengsao, Thailand

---

[1]   Whether Ganesha is younger or older than Kartikeya depends on the region of India. In North India, Ganesha is younger and married, whereas his older brother is unmarried. In South India, Ganesha is older and single, whereas Kartikeya has two wives.

What explains his popularity? It comes from Ganesha's benevolence as the remover of obstacles, for Hindus believe every major undertaking in life is fraught with unknowns. Donald Rumsfeld, then George W. Bush's widely unpopular secretary of defense, famously declared, "There are known knowns; there are known unknowns; and there are unknown unknowns." But even thousands of years before Rumsfeld uttered those words, Hindus were calling upon Ganesha to deal with the unwanted unknowns that manifested as obstacles in their journey. Buying a home, starting a company, writing a book, and purchasing a car—all key moments in life are embarked upon with Ganesha's blessing. Because of his significance in everyday life, he holds a special place among his devotees and is worshipped frequently. Images of Ganesha appear not only in temples and home shrines but at office desks and in bedrooms. He can even be seen hiding in cupboards or the glove compartment of automobiles.

Many stories abound about the origin of Ganesha. In one popular tale, Ganesha is said to have been created because of Parvati's frustration with her husband Shiva. After Shiva repeatedly intrudes in her bath, Parvati decides it's no longer safe to have a bath when he's around. This goes on for days until she has an idea. With the scurf collected from her body, she creates a son and makes him her gatekeeper. When Shiva attempts to burst into her bath again, the newly appointed gatekeeper stops Shiva and drives him away with a cane that leaves a few cuts on Shiva's body. A furious Shiva retaliates by chopping off the head of the stubborn guard, not realizing the gatekeeper was his own son. Parvati is filled with sorrow, but Shiva consoles her by replacing the head of the gatekeeper with that of an elephant. Thus Ganesha got stuck with an elephant head early in his life.

Condemnation was universal for Shiva at his clumsy job of reviving Ganesha with an elephant head. This was not the first time Shiva suffered disapprobation. On another occasion Shiva had revived his father-in-law with a goat's head after decapitating him in a fit of anger. As the deity of destruction, Shiva never really understood the intricacies of creation. Even India's conservative prime minister Narendra Modi weighed in on the issue when he remarked that "an ancient plastic surgeon must have attached the head of an elephant on the body of Ganesha." At the next global meeting of gods, a disconsolate Parvati presented her restored son to the assembled dignitaries. When they looked at Ganesha in disbelief, Shiva felt humiliated and apologized to them. He made amends by making Ganesha the leader of *ganas,* the semi-divine followers of Shiva. As a result Ganesha became known as Ganapati (leader of *ganas*), a name commonly used for him in the South, as is Vinayaka.

As a gatekeeper Ganesha is diligent and steadfast, but occasionally he goes too far in the line of duty and inadvertently becomes an obstacle himself. The sage Parashurama, a disciple of Shiva, once paid a visit to Shiva in his abode at Mount Kailash. Ganesha stopped Parashurama at the gate and refused him entry because Shiva was taking his siesta. A fight promptly ensued. Ganesha used his long trunk to pick up Parashurama and gave him a massive twirl until he was dizzy. When Parashurama came to his senses, he flung his mighty ax at Ganesha, who at once recognized the ax because Shiva had given it to Parashurama. Since Ganesha was an obedient son, he did not insult his father by resisting the weapon. But the ax broke one of his tusks—which is why he's always depicted with a broken tusk.

As is common in Hindu mythology, a different version of the story gives a different reason for Ganesha's broken tusk. It is said that the author-sage Vyasa asked Ganesha to write down the epic Mahabharata, while he dictated the story to him. Knowing the magnitude of the task, Ganesha realized that any ordinary writing tool would be inadequate for the task, so he broke one of his own tusks to create a pen. That is why writers invoke Ganesha as a patron of letters. They also often dedicate their work to Ganesha.

Pictures of Ganesha usually show a rat near his foot as if the poor creature had wandered into the scene. It's customary for Hindu gods to have a mount for transportation that does not depend on fossil fuel, and the rat is Ganesha's vehicle. It may seem odd that while Shiva rides a bull, and Parvati a lion, the portly Ganesha travels around on a measly rat. But that does not mean Ganesha is a second-class citizen. On the contrary,

Ganesha is an intelligent god and smart enough to know his limitations, as the following story attests. Parvati once arranged a race between her two sons, Ganesha and Kartikeya, to determine who was the fastest. Each was asked to go around the world in the shortest time. The strong Kartikeya strutted off in his peacock, confident he would circle the globe faster, but on reaching home he was astounded to learn that his brother had already completed the race. Ganesha won without leaving the room. All he did was to circle around his mother and plead endearingly, "You are my world!" which melted Parvati's heart and clinched the prize for him.

Ganesha's ingenious approach to problem solving has been duplicated on many occasions, including, in recent times, at the 2017 Miss World beauty pageant, held in China. When asked which profession in the world deserved the highest salary and why, a contestant responded, "Mothers sacrifice so much for their children … and deserve not only the highest salary but the highest respect and love." With that singular answer, twenty-year-old Manushi Chhillar of India captured the hearts of not only the audience but the judges and was crowned Miss World from a pool of 118 contestants.

Hindus pay respect to their most popular deity by enthusiastically celebrating Ganesha's birthday. Called Ganesha Chaturthi, the festival lasts ten days and is celebrated all over India. It is especially popular in Mumbai, the commercial capital of India. Temples and homes are decorated with leaves and flowers, and a large clay image of Ganesha is created for the occasion. At the end of the festival, devotees bid Ganesha goodbye by carrying his image in a public procession and immersing it in the Arabian Sea.

Before we say farewell to Ganesha and move on to the next deity, one last thing. When you are touring India, the land of Hindu deities, do as the Indians do—that is, get hold of an image of Ganesha so it will ward off obstacles in your path.[2] Don't assume that doing so will bring

---

[2] Many Hindu gods are highly specialized in their fields. While the elephant-headed Ganesha is the obstacle remover, the monkey-headed Hanuman—which we'll learn at another time—is the distress remover.

you only good luck. Trust me, no Hindu god promises this. Rather, they tacitly acknowledge that sometimes the pendulum of life can swing wildly out of control. But keeping the official obstacle remover by your side will give you hope and prepare you mentally in the face of uninvited unknowns.

There are plenty of difficult obstacles in your path.
Don't allow yourself to become one of them.

—RALPH MARSTON, 1907-1967

❖ ❖ ❖

2

The Vedic Age

More than 5000 years ago a group of pastoral people who spoke a variation of the Indo-European language called Sanskrit lived in the nations known today as India, Pakistan, and Afghanistan. Called the Aryans[3] or the "honorable ones," these Vedic people were led in combat by a supreme commander called Indra, who carried out spectacular attacks on their enemies under the stimulus of a drink called soma.

The Vedic people were nature worshippers and were guided by their priests, who composed motivational poetry praising their leaders and deities. These hymns were memorized and passed down orally, generation by generation, until 800 BCE when they became available in written form. The collection of 1,028 hymns constitutes the Rigveda, one of the sacred books of the Hindus and often considered the earliest collection of poems in any language.[4]

---

[3] The Vedic people were called Aryans, but the word *Aryan* today evokes the anti-Semitism of Hitler's Germany. For that reason, it will be used minimally and only in the Vedic context.

[4] As we'll describe later, the Vedas is of a collection of books, which also includes the Rigveda.

India and neighboring countries

No one knows for certain when the Vedic age began or ended. Although most scholars believe it lasted from 1500 BCE to 500 BCE, some positions of the stars mentioned in the Vedas could have occurred only between 3500 BCE and 4000 BCE, which would mean they are older than what most scholars think. The Vedic age, regarded as the heroic age of Indian civilization, was also the period in which most basic features of the civilization were forged. These include the emergence of Hinduism as the leading religion of India and the social structure called caste.

The Aryans are credited with introducing Sanskrit, the language of the Indian scriptures and mother of most Indian languages, including Hindi. Sanskrit is also the root of Urdu and Sinhala, the national languages of Pakistan and Sri Lanka. Whether the Aryans were indigenous to India or nomads who migrated from the semidry steppes of Russia is still a matter of great controversy and intense debate. The Rigveda provides an important clue—the Saraswati River, which firmly placed their antecedents to the subcontinent. We'll describe this later in the book.

The Rigveda also dedicates several hymns to the Vedic deities from whom a dizzying array of mythology evolved. It is said that India's fascination with mythology is like Britain's obsession with its royals. Endless in scope, the stories of the Vedic gods and goddesses have permeated every level of Indian society and continue to be part of the living culture. In this book we journey into the Vedic world and meet the legends who once ruled the skies of the Vedic era and still live joyfully in the hearts of many Indians.

The Veda was the most precious gift for which the West had ever been indebted to the East.

—FRANÇOIS VOLTAIRE, 1694-1778

❖ ❖ ❖

3

Namaste from Ganesha

This is Ganesha, your flight attendant, speaking. Yes, the chubby elephant-headed fellow you met in the first chapter. You know a bit of my background by now. As the official obstacle remover, I appear in every adventure. You see, life was easy for me, and my protruding belly bears the evidence. But I am here for a different reason, as I want to tell you something about the journey we are about to commence.

As the saying goes, "Forewarned is forearmed." If you are venturing into Hindu mythology for the first time, expect a few jerks and bumps. Chances are you won't crash, but anyone stepping into the ocean of Indian mythology will soon find that the water gets deep pretty fast, for the sheer number of characters is overwhelming. And many come with

Ganesha

multiple personalities and appear and reappear in many forms in the various traditions of the religion. Their combined stories can easily fill state libraries. To complicate matters, some names can be unforgiving and challenging to remember. Even the name of our flight captain, Achuthananda, can be a tongue twister for many. Indians dismiss these objections as lack of familiarity with India or its culture. They point out that if you think Hindu names are overwhelming, take a look at the deities of Buddhism, which cause even smug Indians to stumble.

Believe me, the heavens were not overcrowded in ancient times. A book about the gods would have been as thick as one about the presidents of India. (Since independence in 1947, India has had only a handful of presidents.) In olden times there were a few nature gods, but over time they multiplied through associations, mergers, acquisitions, and joint ventures. Look at me. I was originally a village god with a small following and lived in obscurity, but with the ascent of Shiva I became increasingly popular. By the way, Shiva is sometimes spelled as Śiva and Krishna as *Kṛṣṇa* in popular literature. Rendering Indian spellings in the Roman alphabet has always been a nuisance for writers and readers alike. This book avoids diacritical marks, which attempt to mimic the letters used in the original text. So when you see *sh* and *ch,* they suggest the actual pronunciation: for example, *Uṣas* becomes *Ushas,* and *Ćola* (the ancient dynasty of southern India) is spelled as *Chola,* thereby eliminating any association with a popular soda.

Despite the overabundance of deities, most gods are introduced sequentially in this book. You will have plenty of opportunities to meet, acquaint, or even socialize with them. Yet occasionally you will find major deities like Shiva and Parvati (my parents, in case you have forgotten) arriving with no introduction. Such is the plethora of gods that introductions are not always possible.

As you peruse the book, you will come across many ancient tales that may interest you. Not all are thrillers that will keep you on the edge of your seat. In fact some can barely be called entertaining. We'll be touring olden caves and mountains and then scrutinizing ancient paintings and sculpture. Don't know much about paintings and art? Doesn't matter—I don't have a degree either. I'll have you singing many little songs and dancing many little dances together. Sometimes you will be thrilled—or saddened—yet it's a journey every lover of mythology and culture should take.

Although the West has coveted India's fabrics, cuisine, labor, and talent over the years, India's greatest gift to the world has been its mythology. There were no Olympic sprinters or swimmers or gymnasts. The whole country was tuned in to the mythology channel. Great explorers like Magellan and Marco Polo undertook many voyages to discover the world, but the ancient seers of India discovered the universe from the highest states of mediation—without leaving their caves or rooms. These timeless truths were then wrapped with mythological tales for the benefit of humanity.

So let's get started. It's time to fasten your seat belts. Keep your ears tuned and eyes peeled. Do you need to bring anything for this trip? All I ask of you during this journey is an appreciation of ancient culture. Just as you will discover gold, you will also find plenty of dirt. This is why Indians endearingly refer to their motherland as "Mera Bharat Mahan" meaning "my great India," but often alluding to the fact that anything—good or bad—can be found in the country. That said, as the obstacle remover, my job is to eliminate the hurdles in your path—regardless of what you are looking for. Off we go! Sach will take over from me now.

> *The real voyage of discovery consists not in seeking new landscapes, but in having new eyes.*
>
> —MARCEL PROUST, 1871-1922

❖ ❖ ❖

4

How Varuna Became
the God of the Oceans

From a distance the sea appears serene and peaceful, but sailors know that the mighty ocean at times shows no generosity. Before embarking on a sea voyage, Hindus pray to Varuna, the ruler of the ocean, a practice that continues today, although not many people realize that Varuna, whose powers eroded through the centuries, was once the supreme ruler of the universe, [5] including the oceans.

One of the oldest gods of the Hindu pantheon, Varuna was the highest ranking deity at the peak of his powers. He was the king of the gods and the guardian of Rta,[6] or the sacred laws. The name Varuna is derived from *var,* which in Sanskrit means "to cover." As the god of the universe, he oversees everything. Varuna makes the sun shine in the heavens. His

---

[5] The universe in Vedic times had three parts: sky (heaven), middle air, and earth. The three parts are sometimes referred to as the three worlds.

[6] Rta is usually translated as cosmic order, such as the regular occurrence of day and night, seasons, and the like. However, Rta also includes ethical and ritualistic order.

breath is the wind. Using his supernatural power, or *maya,* [7] he causes the rain to fall and rivers to flow, thereby sustaining his creatures.

Varuna has many qualities, but his omniscience makes him exceptional. He sits majestically in his thousand-columned, thousand-gated golden palace in the sky, where he is accompanied by his vigilant spies, including the sun and the stars. He is said to know the flight of birds in the sky, the course of the far-traveling wind, the paths of ships on the ocean, and much more.

Varuna on his mount, Makara, in a 17th century Bundi painting

Varuna is depicted as a white god with four arms who rides a crocodile called Makara. On his right hand he carries a noose with which he performs his role as the cosmic hangman. His usual technique is to lasso the offender with the noose, although Varuna can be forgiving at times.

---

[7] *Maya* has many meanings, including delusion (Advaita Vedanta). Here it means the cosmic energy of the Supreme Being—which some scholars call magic.

He is known to extend the lives of the good and shorten the lives of those who violate the Rta. That is why Varuna is known as the judgmental god, providing justice as well as meting out punishment.

Occasionally he is called the lord of the dead, a position he shares with Yama, and Varuna is able to confer immortality to those who seek his pardon. Varuna has an ethical side, and among the Vedic deities he has higher moral standing than any other god. He is often called the ethical god, and people call upon him for fairness and forgiveness.

You will be surprised to learn that Varuna was originally an *asura* (demon) in the Rigveda, the holy book of Hindus. The later parts of the text address him as a *deva* (demigod), probably because of the negative connotations that became attached to *asuras* over time. The Rigveda, for that matter, was originally transmitted orally and only later compiled and written down. Varuna's reign at the top, however, was short-lived. A demon called Vritra kept the cosmic waters captive, and the lack of rain brought drought and widespread famine. Varuna, as the protector of the universe, fought alongside Indra to retrieve the waters, but it was Indra who slayed the demon, destroying Vritra's ninety-nine fortresses and releasing the waters. After this heroic act Indra gained recognition as the top god. Varuna was sidelined as the guardian of the waters. His palace was relocated to a mountain called Pushpagiri, which lies beneath the waters. Varuna still carries the noose but also totes an umbrella formed by the hood of a cobra.

Varuna's moral standing also took a turn for the worse. The Mahabharata relates that Varuna fell deeply in love with the beautiful Bhadra, who also happened to be the wife of the sage Uthathya. The love-struck Varuna abducted Bhadra and hid her under the sea. When the infuriated sage learned what had happened, he drank the entire ocean dry. Varuna's hideout was exposed, and he was forced to return Bhadra.

His troubles did not end there. Once Varuna became infatuated with an *apsara* called Urvashi. The *apsaras* are celestial nymphs and the Vedic equivalents of the Kardashian clan. Varuna is said to have lost control of himself when he saw the enchanting Urvashi and involuntarily discharged his seeds into the heavenly pot—perhaps one of the earliest cases of sexual dysfunction in gods. The result of this mishap was the birth of a son called Agastya. Agastya's birth certificate, however, lists two fathers. It appears that the god Mitra also was distracted by Urvashi and had simultaneously released his seeds. As a result Agastya has two fathers.[8] You would think Agastya, who did not know the identity of his true biological father, would lead a sad life, struggling with identity crisis and suffering from damaged self-esteem. Nothing was further from the truth. Agastya grew up to be one of the eminent sages of India and became the father of Tamil literature. He is also considered the father of traditional Indian medicine.

Although most hymns in the Rigveda are addressed to Indra, a handful are dedicated to Varuna. He is often connected with Uranus, the god of the sky in Greek mythology, and sometimes with Ahura Mazda, the god of the Zoroastrians.

In the Vedic era Indra was unquestionably the greatest of the gods, but he never instilled the awe and fear that Varuna commanded at the time of his glory. But today you will not find any images of Varuna, for no one worships him in temples or home shrines. Seafarers have abandoned him, for they rely on Dhruva[9] for navigational guidance.

But Varuna is not a forgotten god. In the story of Krishna you will learn that he turned to Varuna for help in securing some prime real estate to build his city of Dvaraka. Hindus routinely invoke Varuna during Vedic rituals even today. A small pot containing water, which signifies auspiciousness, is an important part of every Hindu ceremony. Water is also sprinkled and drunk at the beginning of each prayer. Varuna and its variations are popular names in India, and many ships in the Indian navy bear his name.

---

[8] If you are wondering whether it's possible for a child to have two fathers, the answer is yes. It can happen when a woman has sexual intercourse with two men during the same menstrual cycle, and two of her eggs are fertilized separately by each man.

[9] Dhruva was a Vishnu devotee who became immortalized as Pole Star. We describe Dhruva in book 2 of this series.

Varuna is one of the most interesting creations of the Hindu mind, because, though we can still perceive the physical background from which he rises, the vast, starry, brilliant expanse above, his features more than those of any other Vedic god have been completely transfigured, and he stands before us as a god who watches over the world, punishes the evil-doer, and even forgives the sins of those who implore his pardon.

—MAX MULLER, 1823-1900

❋ ❋ ❋

5

Friend, Thy Name Is Mitra

Mitra by himself is hardly known, but together with Varuna, the Mitra-Varuna jodi (pair) is one of the formidable mythological duos of the Vedic times. In their heyday they were as popular as the pairs like Lava-Kusha or Rama-Lakshmana.[10] Together Mitra and Varuna were the custodians of the sacred Vedic laws—Varuna as the guardian of the cosmic order and Mitra as the protector of the human order. As Varuna's executor, Mitra was the enforcer of the cosmic law. Although Mitra earned a reputation for integrity and strict enforcement, he was his subjects' greatest friend when they faced moral dilemmas. He was also the guardian of promises and agreements.

Mitra is sometimes called Varuna's twin or alter ego. Both Varuna and Mitra were important gods during pre-Vedic times. Like Varuna, Mitra was an *asura* who later became a *deva*. And like Varuna, he was one among the twelve Adityas, who were the children of Aditi. While Aditi represented the boundless heaven, her sons represented the twelve signs of the Zodiac and rotated their roles as sun god every month of the year.

---

[10] We discuss in detail Lava-Kusha and Rama-Lakshmana in book 3 of this series.

So Mitra is sometimes attributed with solar characteristics as the spirit of day, but always in relation to Varuna. When Mitra is connected with day, Varuna is the night. When Mitra is the sunrise, Varuna becomes the sunset.

The bromance between Mitra and Varuna existed not only at work but also during leisure. They had identical tastes too. Like Varuna, Mitra was enchanted by the *apsara* Urvashi and fathered the sage Agastya jointly with Varuna. The story doesn't end there. In fact another pair of Mitra-Varuna seeds was released when they glimpsed Urvashi, but missed the heavenly pot and spilled over ground where it was fertilized by Mother Earth. The sage Vasishtha, whose soul at that time was separated from his body because of a curse, used this seed to launch his reentry into the world. Like Agastya, Vasishtha turned out to be one of the greatest sages India produced. He was also a Saptarishi, one of the seven great sages, and was later inducted to the highest class of sages called Brahmarishi. The Mitra-Varuna-Urvashi trio is therefore credited with creating two of the greatest seers of Hinduism.

But this is where the similarities end. While Varuna created awe and fear, Mitra generated intimacy and trust. If Varuna was the military task-master with a noose, Mitra was the friendly spirit who steered people to emulate him and cooperate in their tasks. A measure of Mitra's popularity is the number of hymns dedicated exclusively to him. In the Rigveda only one hymn is addressed to Mitra alone; however, the Mitra-Varuna pair attracts a number of dedications. Whereas Varuna's powers became weaker toward the end of the Vedic age, Mitra's significance eroded so much that he no longer dwelled in the Indian skies. In fact he migrated to Persia, where he was known as Mithra and became the god of light. From Persia Mithra's cult spread all the way to Rome.

Although Mitra is a lost god, Hindus still honor Varuna's friendship with Mitra, for the word *mitra* is a popular term for a friend in most Indian languages. As a solar deity Mitra is also addressed in the concluding part of the Gayatri Mantra, which is a collection of verses that practicing Hindus consider the most sacred.

A real friend is one who walks in when the rest of the world walks out.

—WALTER WINCHELL, 1897-1972

6

Indra – The Greatest of the Vedic Gods

The heavens shuddered and the earth trembled. Prithvi had given birth to another child. There was no rejoicing, only anxiety. She looked at her children for help, but none would come to her aid, for they feared this child would change the divine order and create their own doom. Prithvi had kept the child in her womb for an abnormally long gestation to protect him from a jealous father. She hid her son, as a vulnerable infant, even after his birth so as not to attract attention. But her attempts at concealing the infant were futile as the child began to display a sense of energy rarely seen among newborns. Little did Prithvi realize that she had unleashed a Category 5 storm god called Indra, who would soon become the ruler of the universe.

Indra riding his white elephant, Airavata, in an undated Thiruchirappalli painting

Prithvi, as Mother Earth, and Dyaus Pita as father of the sky, were symbolized as cow and bull[11] and worshipped as fertility gods. As the early deities they were believed to have created the gods and humans.

---

[11] Although Prithvi and Dyaus Pita are acknowledged as Indra's parents, his birth story has many variations. Some latter-day texts refer to Daksha (the primordial male principal of creation) and Aditi (his female counterpart) as Indra's parents. Although Aditi is regarded as the mother of gods (usually gods of Vedic origin like Varuna, Mitra, and Indra), her sons are Adityas, the zodiac signs. Originally the Adityas numbered seven, but their number later increased to twelve. Varuna was the chief Aditya. Early on the Adityas were known as *asuras*. After Indra became top god, the term *asura* was used only for demons.

At the time of Indra's birth, humans were in the midst of severe famine and were pleading with the gods to rescue them. The demon Vritra had taken the form of a serpent and had stolen the clouds, preventing rain from reaching the earth and triggering drought in the region. Unable to bear the sight of Vritra terrorizing people, Indra seized from Tvashtri, the artisan god, the intoxicating drink of soma, which was being offered to the gods, and quaffed a large quantity, which made him grow to the size of a giant. Clutching his thunderbolt Vajra, Indra set out in a chariot drawn by two horses to fight against Vritra. A group of attendants and lowers closely followed Indra. Inspired by the hymns of the priests on earth and strengthened by the sacrifices, Indra stormed and captured Vritra's ninety-nine fortresses and then came face to face with the demon himself. Although Vritra thought himself to be invulnerable, Indra soon found his opponent had some weaknesses. Invigorated by the soma, Indra slayed Vritra with the thunderbolt. The clouds were released and the genial rains descended upon earth, making the land fertile again.

With this act Indra supplanted Varuna as the provider of rain, but Indra did not stop there. His next act was to attack his own father, who preferred his other sons to Indra. It is said that Dyaus deliberately kept Indra away from soma, the source of this son's strength. With one swift motion Indra seized Dyaus by the ankle and dashed him to the ground, killing him instantaneously.[12] By destroying Dyaus, Indra set the stage for his independence and full stature as a god.

Indra is relentless in his opposition to demons. He also defends people and animals from the ploys of other demons, including Vritra's mother, Danu,[13] who was killed with his thunderbolt. Soon Indra became the ruler of the universe, comprising the heavens, the middle air, and earth. He gradually took over Varuna's other functions as fertility god and creator god. While Varuna's power was based on cosmic law and *maya,* Indra's strength came from his physical prowess and spiritual deeds.

---

[12] There is some confusion in the literature about the motive for killing.

[13] Danu is the mother of the Danava race of asuras.

Indra was undoubtedly the greatest of the Vedic gods. No phenomenon of nature is as ruthless as the lightning strike. Most Rigvedic hymns are dedicated to Indra. He is often associated with Zeus, the sky god in Greek mythology, and with Jupiter in Roman mythology.[14] In pictures Indra is often represented as a man with a ruddy complexion and four arms and hands. He uses two hands to hold a lance, the third to hold his famous thunderbolt, and the fourth is empty. Indra is sometimes called "the thousand-eyed" and pictured with only two arms but with eyes all over his body.

The seven-headed flying horse, Uchchaichsravas, painting ca. 1800 by an unknown artist

Although Indra is known to have an active, bellicose disposition, often riding a chariot during his conquests or his wonderful horse,

---

[14] Dyaus Pita may seem to be the Vedic equivalent of Zeus, but Indra gradually superseded Dyaus in Hindu worship. Zeus and Indra had striking similarities in their birth, appearance, romances, and adventures.

Uchchaihsravas,[15] he becomes a less active and more dignified ruler in the latter part of the Vedic period. He is pictured as reigning in the heavens from the capital city of Amaravati on Mount Meru and flanked by his queen, Indrani. He has abandoned his horse; instead he is shown riding a white elephant called Airavata. In his palace reside the celestial nymphs, or *apsaras,* and in the palace gardens grows the all-yielding tree Parijata, whose fragrant flowers would later create a rift between Indra and Krishna.

❖ ❖ ❖

---

[15] Uchchaihsravas is a snow white, seven-headed flying horse and is said to be the king of horses. He is often described as the mount of Indra and of Bali, the demon king.

7

Indra's Fall from Grace

As king of the universe, Indra held the highest rank in the Vedas, but his reign did not last long. In the Brahmanic times (900–600 BCE),[16] Indra's ranking plummeted to that of a secondary god, behind the supreme Hindu triad of Brahma (the creator god), Vishnu (the god responsible for maintenance of the universe), and Shiva (the destroyer god). It is even said that Indra is not a god but the title of the highest executive level position in the heavens appointed by the supreme triad and approved by other celestial deities. The position is awarded every thousand years to a god or man who can ascend to that status by performing one hundred sacrifices. As the king of celestials, Indra still rides the white elephant with his consort, Indrani, but instead of being the object of worship, he can now be seen worshipping Shiva, Parvati, and Ganesha.'

---

[16] Although the Vedas was transmitted orally more than five thousand years ago, the Vedic age is usually considered 1500–500 BCE when the four Vedas were written down. The period of 900–600 BCE is known as the Brahmanic period when the Brahmanas, which focus on rituals, were composed. The priestly class became powerful during the Brahmanic period.

Indra is no longer the lord of the universe, but he remains the king of the heavens. He still wages constant war against the demons, but his victories are no longer guaranteed. The Brahmanic age forged not only a regime change in the heavens but revisions to the belief system. The power of the Brahmin priestly class grew stronger, and sacrifice became an important part of the religious ritual. The priests put an end to the sanctity of binge drinking. Under the new beliefs, power is obtained not by drinking huge quantities of soma but by performing sacrifices or engaging in austerities to appease the supreme triad. Just as good behavior was rewarded with boons, perpetrators were punished with curses. These changes evened up the odds for the demons in their never-ending battles against the gods, because the demons had never been permitted to drink soma. The demons were, however, exceptionally good at appeasing the gods.

In the Brahmanic age murder of a Brahmin[17] by anyone outside the caste was considered a crime. The slaying of the demon Vritra, which until then had been recognized as a heroic act, became a criminal act because of Vritra's Brahmin ancestry. Indra belonged to the Kshatriya caste and was therefore found guilty. To atone for his crime, Indra was made to leave heaven. While Indra was away, a certain earthly king called Nahusha performed sacrifices and succeeded Indra on the throne. Once in power, Nahusha became infatuated with Indrani and sought her company. The sensuous Indrani, however, stood by her husband and sought advice from Brihaspati, the advisor of gods. On Brihaspati's advice Indrani agreed to accept Nahusha as her husband if he arrived in full regal glory in a palanquin carried by the Saptarishis, the seven great sages. Nahusha's plan was, however, foiled by a freak incident after Agastya, one of the bearers of his palanquin, became annoyed when the impatient Nahusha kept goading him to walk faster. Agastya put a curse on him, and Nahusha tumbled down to earth as a serpent. He was liberated much later by the Pandavas of the Mahabharata.

---

[17] Brahmin is priestly class of the Hindus and not related to Brahma, the creator god in the supreme triad, or Brahman, the ultimate reality in Hinduism.

Another king who extended his control of the three worlds by appeasing the gods was the demon Bali, who was arrogant but generous to his people. When he defeated Indra and expelled him from heaven, the gods felt challenged and, fearing Bali's growing powers, pleaded with Vishnu to limit Bali's influence. At their request Vishnu transformed himself into a dwarf called Vamana[18] and approached Bali, who was performing a *yajna* (sacrifice), and asked for a simple gift—three paces of land. Bali granted the wish without much thought. Vamana then increased his stature to his true cosmic form, and in the first of three famous steps, he covered the sky, which blotted out the stars, and the earth with the second. Bali realized that Vamana had no place for the last step and, as a demon of his word, offered his head. Before Vishnu banished Bali to the netherworld, he granted Bali a boon that allowed him to return from exile every year to visit his kingdom and people.[19]

The ten-headed Ravana, the demon king of Lanka and the central villain in the epic Ramayana, was yet another king who humiliated Indra under the new belief system. When the forces of Ravana, whose prodigious power was derived from his Brahmin ancestry and religious sacrifices, marched against Indra, the king of the gods found himself utterly incapable of defending the heavens. Ravana's warrior son Meghanada apprehended Indra, tied him up, and took him to Lanka, where he was held hostage along with other gods. At the palace the hostages were assigned household chores befitting their background and experience. Thus Agni became a cook and prepared food for Ravana, Varuna carried the water, Kubera handled the finances, and Vayu, the wind god, swept the floors of the palace. While Shiva became a busy barber shaving beard from Ravana's ten heads, Indra suffered the humiliation of being a

---

[18] Vamana is the fifth reincarnation (avatar) of Vishnu. Book 3 of this series deals with Vamana in more detail.

[19] The homecoming of King Bali is celebrated every year as the festival of Onam, when the Indian state of Kerala pays glorious tribute to the memory of this benign demon who loved his subjects.

Vamana with King Bali (Calcutta Art Studio ca. 1880)

domestic servant. To secure their release, Brahma and other gods headed to Lanka, where negotiations began in earnest. Finally, Brahma offered Meghanada the title of Indrajit, which means conqueror of Indra, and the demon accepted gladly. But Meghanada was a shrewd negotiator and demanded a bigger ransom—total immortality, which Brahma declined, saying that it is against the law of nature. The deadlock was broken when Brahma granted a boon to Meghanada that he could never be defeated in battle so long as he was able to perform *yajna* before combat.

Although Indra was the greatest of the gods and the inspiration for such words as *Indranet* and *Indrajala*, he is not worshipped by the masses, a fact that frustrates him and makes him jealous of other gods, including Krishna. It is said that Indra deliberately caused torrential rains in Gokula, where Krishna spent his childhood, to create havoc and teach devotees a lesson as they worshipped Krishna instead of him. To humble Indra, Krishna lifted Mount Govardhana on his fingertips and sheltered the people under it for seven days until Indra relented. This was also when Krishna established his authority over the *devas* (demigods).

Indra and Krishna were at loggerheads again over a tree. Krishna, accompanied by his wife, Satyabhama, once paid a visit to Indra at his palace. Satyabhama spotted a beautiful tree adorned with fragrant flowers and luscious fruit in the garden. This was the Parijata tree produced at the churning of the ocean. According to legend, wearing the flowers of the tree allows a wife to preserve the love of her husband, and eating its fruit allows people to recall their previous existences. Satyabhama fell in love with the tree and wanted to take it to her home in Dvaraka. At his wife's request Krishna uprooted the tree and placed it on Garuda, his bird vehicle. Suddenly the heavens were in turmoil as Indra and his attendants protested the removal of the tree. A fight ensued. Despite his strength in numbers, Indra was outmaneuvered. In a final attempt to overcome Krishna, Indra hurled his thunderbolt, but Krishna caught it like a Frisbee. Nothing and no one could best Krishna, and he returned home unhurt and planted the tree in his garden.

The Brahmanic period made significant changes to the landscape of Hinduism. As the Brahmins became influential, the caste system became embedded in the culture. But their large-scale animal sacrifices and their pretensions to superiority by virtue of their birth engendered opposition.

Although austerity and asceticism became widely popular practices during this period, several reform movements, like Buddhism and Jainism, began to challenge these practices. Hinduism responded to these challenges, but the Brahmanic period had already laid the foundation for a social framework based on hierarchical classes that would remain entrenched for many centuries.

8

The Moral Decadence of Indra

Despite slaying Vritra and earning the sobriquet Vritrahan, Indra could no longer be counted on to win battles, for his reputation as a warrior god had greatly diminished after the Vedic period. Soma, the source of Indra's strength in the Vedic period, now was seen as the reason for his physical weakness and moral laxity. The traits once perceived as boldness and courage came to be viewed as impulsiveness or behavior characterized by little thought about the consequences. As lord of the heavens, Indra needed new tactics to deal with both the demons' constant incursions into his territory and the threat posed by the ascetics, who had become powerful through penance and austerity. Trickery and deceit became the order of the day.

Much is written about Indra's moral decadence in the later times. As the lord of heaven, he chose his wife, Shachi, the daughter of the demon Puloman, not for her ability to cook delicious Indian meals but for her overwhelming sensuality over the dazzling *apsaras* in heaven. Such was her sensuality that a huge virile ape called Vrishakapi once extolled her fleshy hips during his stay at Indra's abode. Legend has it that under the influence of soma, Indra became attracted to the voluptuous Shachi and imposed his will without her consent. On hearing this, Puloman became enraged and was about to cast a curse, when Indra killed him. Although Shachi, as Indrani,[20] remained his queen and stood by her god even during his darkest hours, Indra embarked on a series of love affairs, mostly with married women.

As the king of the universe, Indra operated without a road map and showed little reluctance about misusing his power, particularly in regard to women. He was guilty of the greatest immorality in attempting to seduce Ahalya, the wife of his spiritual teacher Gautama. She was alone at the hermitage when Indra entered the house and began professing his love. A flattered Ahalya was about to yield to his wishes when her husband returned home only to find Indra making advances to his wife. He put a curse on Indra that his body would always bear one thousand marks of the yoni (vagina). Like many sages before him, Gautama later relented and amended the curse, changing the thousand marks of disgrace into a thousand eyes. But Indra was undeterred in his passion for Ahalya. With the help of Chandra, the moon god, who took the form of a rooster and crowed at midnight, Indra managed to lure Gautama out of his house to perform his morning prayers. Indra then assumed the form of a sage and took Gautama's place beside Ahalya in bed. When Gautama returned home, he found his wife united in *maithuna* with an unidentified bearded man who looked like the sage's own mirror image. It didn't take a giant leap to figure out the identity of the intruder upon which the sage interrupted their *maithuna*. "But I was deceived into this act," protested Ahalya. Gautama was in no mood to listen to excuses and issued fresh curses for both, setting them back in their reincarnation cycles. Ahalya was turned into a stone, and Indra became a eunuch. Ahalya had to wait several years before Rama, the hero of the epic Ramayana, restored her to her original self. For Indra redemption came much sooner. After he performed a sacrifice, the gods forgave and rescued him.

---

[20] Indrani refers to Indra's queen.

Indra often called upon the stunning *apsaras*[21] in his palace to tempt ascetics, whose growing power was threatening the dominion of the gods. It is said that the power gained by doing penance is far greater than that from physical might. One such ascetic was the famous sage Vishwamitra, much revered in texts for composing the Gayatri Mantra and who for many years was known for his extreme austerity. An *apsara* called Menaka was sent to seduce Vishwamitra and disrupt his meditation. As Menaka approached Vishwamitra, the wind god Vayu gently disrobed her and the ensuing wardrobe malfunction disrupted the sage's concentration. The air crackled with extreme lightning and thunder as Indra led the gods in rejoicing.

Soon thereafter Menaka gave birth to a child. The sage was dismayed that he had lost the virtue gained through many years of penance. "What! my wisdom, my austerities, my firm resolutions, all destroyed at once by a woman? Seduced by the crime in which Indra delights I am stripped of the advantages arising from my penances!"[22] Vishwamitra did not put a curse on Menaka, but he distanced himself from the child,[23] who was left abandoned on the banks of a river. Years later Vishwamitra got his chance at redemption when Indra sent Rambha, the queen of *apsaras,* to disturb his meditation. The sage did not swallow the bait this time. He cursed Rambha and turned her into a stone for a thousand years.

Like Menaka, not all *apsaras* were successful in the art of seduction. Indra once invited his son Arjuna, the protagonist of both the Mahabharata and the Bhagavad Gita, to his palace. Upon Arjuna's arrival, Indra found his usually collected son utterly riveted by Urvashi, who was dancing in the court. This was the same Urvashi who caused sexual dysfunction in many heavenly oglers like Varuna and Mitra. When Indra

---

[21] Apsaras are known for their sensuality and dancing skills. They are often the wives of the Gandharvas, the court musicians of Indra. The most famous apsaras are Urvashi, Menaka, Rambha, and Tilottama.

[22] Edward Moor in his book Hindu Pantheon

[23] The abandoned child survived and became Shakuntala, who later became the mother of King Bharata, from whom India (Bharat) gets its name.

noticed that his son was smitten by the charms of Urvashi, he offered her to his son. That evening, per Indra's instructions, Urvashi, decorated in jewelry and dressed in the most provocative outfit, came to Arjuna's quarters. Arjuna opened the door and embraced her warmly. He spoke glowingly about her forefathers and his admiration for her. As the progenitor of the Kuru family, Urvashi was like a mother to him. As the conversation progressed, Urvashi realized that Arjuna had motherly affection toward her, not physical attraction. But rejection was hard for the *apsara* to deal with as she felt insulted that a mere mortal was able to resist her. Urvashi put a curse on Arjuna, turning him into a eunuch for the rest of his life—but Indra intervened and reduced the curse to one year.

Of the Vedic gods, Indra was the most popular, with about one-fourth of Vedic hymns dedicated to him. Despite his character flaws (which were mostly exposed by the Puranic writers of later times), Hindus remember him for his courage and leadership. Unlike Vishnu, Shiva, or Krishna, he is not universally worshipped, but people still pay homage to him in some parts of India, especially in seasons of drought. Monikers for Indra, such as Mahendra and Sakra, are still popular in India, as are the many variations of his name, such as Surendra, Ravindra, Jitendra, and the like.[24]

From Indra we get the metaphor of Indra's net, or Indranet, which is a net that hangs over his palace in Mount Meru but was designed by some ingenious artificer so that the net stretches infinitely in all directions. At each vertex is mounted a jewel that reflects all other jewels and is in turn reflected in all the other jewels. Indra used the Indranet as a tactical net to snare his enemies in his unrelenting effort to drive away demons.[25] From Hinduism the concept of Indranet permeated to Buddhism, where it is used to describe the interconnectedness of the universe.

---

[24] Mahendra comes from Sanskrit, meaning "Great Indra [god]." Similarly, Surendra is lord of gods, Ravindra is sun god (Surya), and Jitendra is the conqueror of Indra (god) and a synonym for Indrajit.

[25] This technique of catching his enemies by using the Indranet is often referred to as *Indrajala,* a Sanskrit word meaning sorcery or magic.

The idea of Indranet has been explored and applied in places far beyond the realm of eastern religions. About 3000 years after the concept of Indranet was described in the Atharvaveda, the modern Internet was invented. The two events are not connected, of course, but when we think of computers as replacements for the jewels at each vertex of the Indranet, we can see that the infinite net once used to snare people has become a net to connect people.

❖ ❖ ❖

9

Parade of the Ants

Shortly after Indra defeated Vritra and became the king of gods, an arrogant Indra ordered the heavenly craftsman Vishwakarma (also known as Tvashtri) to build him a palace befitting the king of gods. Vishwakarma built him a magnificent residence with elegant quarters and tall towers that was surrounded by gardens and lakes. But Indra was not satisfied. He wanted larger rooms, spacious corridors, taller towers, and more. In fact his endless demand for extensions and pavilions was so exhausting that Vishwakarma sought the help of Brahma, who in turn appealed to Vishnu for mediation.

Soon Vishnu visited Indra's palace disguised as a Brahmin boy and praised Indra's new palace, saying that no former Indra could have built such a marvel. At first the child's remark amuses Indra, but soon he is horrified as the boy narrates the chronicles of former Indras against the great cycles of creation and destruction. A procession of ants enters the hall, and the boy reveals the ants are former Indras, whose past misdeeds gradually turned them into ants. Meanwhile another visitor enters the hall. It is Shiva, disguised as a hermit with a hairy chest that has a circular bald spot. Shiva reveals that each of his chest hairs corresponds to the life of one Indra. Each time a hair falls, one Indra dies and another replaces him.

Shocked by the revelation, Indra releases Vishwakarma from any further work on the palace. Cured of extreme ambition, Indra becomes a changed man, no longer caring about his riches. As Indra prepares to relinquish his worldly life, his wife, Shachi, summons Brihaspati, who teaches Indra how to appreciate the virtues of both spiritual and worldly life. In the end Indra learns how to pursue wisdom while fulfilling his kingly duties.

Although the parade of ants was meant to show how Indra lost his boundless pride, it also reinforces the Hindu concepts of karma and reincarnation. Life is, according to Hinduism, a giant Ferris wheel, rotating ad infinitum with one rotation equivalent to a life span. You begin life as the wheel rotates upward and reach full adulthood when the wheel reaches the zenith. Old age sets in on the downward journey and death lies at the end. The body is gone, but the soul lives on. The cycle doesn't stop. Depending on the karmic credits you've earned, you begin the next ride in another form of life with another opportunity to earn karmic credits. The meaning of life is not to go around the wheel endlessly but to achieve *moksha* and escape from the cycle of reincarnation.

❂ ❂ ❂

10

Dadhichi's Supreme Sacrifice

The good and the great are only separated by their willingness to sacrifice.

—KAREEM ABDUL-JABBAR, 1947-

In Sanskrit *vajra* can mean both thunderbolt and diamond. Mythology-attuned Hindus will at once point out that the Vajra is the weapon of Indra, the Vedic lord of the heavens. Indeed the Vajra can be a weapon with both the indestructible power of a diamond and the irresistible force of the thunderbolt. As a weapon it resembles a club with a ribbed spherical head. Depictions of Indra often show him riding an elephant while holding the Vajra. A remarkable story about the Vajra forms the background of India's highest military award. According to Hindu mythology, Indra received the Vajra because of a supreme sacrifice made by the sage Dadhichi.

As the fortunes kept fluctuating at the heavens, Indra once found himself at the receiving end when the gods were terrorized by the demon Vritra, who through severe penance obtained a boon that gave him immunity from death by any known weapon of that time. This was when Vritra

Vajra, Indra's thunderbolt

took the form of a serpent, enveloped a celestial mountain, and stole the clouds, causing drought in the region. Worse still, Vritra's powers grew with each battle and soon he threw Indra out of the heavens. With no hope of recovering his kingdom, Indra approached Brahma, who directed him to Vishnu. After considerable thought, Vishnu revealed that only a weapon made from the bones of the sage Dadhichi could kill Vritra.

Indra was in a quandary. He had once beheaded the sage for revealing the secret of Madhu-vidya to the Ashvin twins, the physicians of the gods. Madhu-vidya had the power to restore a person from the dead, and the Ashvins used this secret to revive the sage at that time. Yet Indra longed to recoup his power and position. Reluctantly, he went to Naimisaranya, the forest where the sage lived, and asked for his assistance. The eminent Dadhichi was not the type to hold a grudge. He was more big-hearted than the gods themselves and mused, "This body will wither anyway. If it can serve any useful purpose, so be it." The sage, however, had one small wish. Before he gave up his life, he wanted to embark on a pilgrimage to all the holy rivers. Since such a pilgrimage would take considerable time, Indra used his magical powers to bring all the holy waters to Naimisaranya, which allowed the sage to fulfill his wish at once. Dadhichi is said to have left his body through his yogic powers. Thereafter the *devas* fashioned the Vajra, Indra's thunderbolt weapon, from the sage's thighbone. A fierce battle soon ensued between Vritra, the marauding serpent, and Indra, who, clutching the powerful

Vajra, split the serpent's stomach, which killed him, ending his tyranny and releasing the waters.

A variation of the same story goes back to the time when the gods and the demons were observing a truce. At this time the gods wanted to hide their weapons so that they would not fall into the hands of the demons. So the gods went to Dadhichi's hermitage in the forest and asked him to safeguard their weapons—which the sage did gladly. All of a sudden the heavens experienced an unusually long period of peace, so long that the weapons slowly started losing their power. With no claimants for the weapons, Dadhichi dissolved them in sacred water and drank it, empowering his bones. But as soon as he finished drinking the water, the gods were back asking for their weapons. Dadhichi felt obligated to honor their request. He realized that his bones were the only means for the gods to defeat the demons, and he willingly gave up his life in a pit of mystical flames. Brahma is said to have then fashioned a large number of weapons, including the Vajra, which was created from his thighbone.

In reverence for Dadhichi's ultimate sacrifice in the fight of good against evil, India has made the Param Vir Chakra its highest military honor. It is equivalent to the Medal of Honor in the United States or the Victoria Cross in the United Kingdom. Param Vir Chakra means "wheel of the ultimate brave" and recognizes sacrifice as the ultimate expression of patriotism. It is awarded for the highest degree of gallantry, often posthumously to soldiers killed in combat.

❂ ❂ ❂

11

The Power of Mythology

Until 1000 CE, Greece and Rome were the only nations in Europe telling stories of heroes and victors. England was just a dreary little island inhabited by castoffs, barbarians, whiners, and losers. Hoping to instill a sense of pride in his countrymen, a Welsh monk called Geoffrey of Monmouth prepared a complete history of England and published it in 1136 CE. Titled *History of the Kings of Britain*, Geoffrey's work was a detailed written account chronicling the deeds of the English people over 2000 years that painted them with a glorious and distinguished heritage. There was one problem: Not a single word of it was true. Yet by creating the mythological tales of Merlyn, Guinevere, Arthur, and the Knights of the Round Table from the fabric of imagination, Geoffrey persuaded his countrymen to see themselves as heroes and victors from a wonderful nation.

After Geoffrey's work was published, the British went on to explore, conquer, and rule much of the world for hundreds of years. It became the largest empire in history and, for more than a century, was the foremost global power. The adage "the sun never sets on the British empire" was true until 1937 when England had possessions in each of the world's twenty-four time zones – including their most valued and prized possession, India.

By colonizing India, the British awakened a sleeping giant whose tales and stories were mightier and more numerous than theirs. In India the mythological heroes of both countries fought against each other. The British folklore was like a drop in the vast ocean of even older Hindu mythology. Ten years later the British left India, never to return. Tales of King Arthur and Merlyn were buried by stories about Shiva and Krishna from a country whose mythology had been evolving for more than five thousand years. Today India is 82 percent Hindu, despite countless attempts over the centuries to convert its people to Christianity. The Hindu fables were more entertaining and fantastic than Geoffrey's collection of quasi-historic tales—and the Indians steadfastly clung to theirs for thousands of years.

Most people assume that legends and myths are simply the by-products of a great civilization. Actually the contrary is true. Historically the greatest civilizations have been those with stories of heroes and role models who inspired ordinary people to do incredible things. Stories of Durga and Rama and Krishna have been making the rounds for thousands of years on the subcontinent. Famous people like Mahatma Gandhi, Rabindranath Tagore, Swami Vivekananda, and Jawaharlal Nehru were merely ordinary people energized by the tales of Indian mythology.

Mythology and science both extend the scope of human beings. Like science and technology, mythology is not about opting out of this world, but about enabling us to live more intensely within it.

—KAREN ARMSTRONG, 1944-

12

Agni – The Fire God

Have you been to that colorful and cultural extravaganza called an Indian wedding? Often packed into a week of lavish celebrations and abundant food, Indian weddings typically have an extremely long list of invitees. Although Indian weddings are, by and large, arranged marriages, it is a little known fact that arranged marriages are more a cultural phenomenon than a religious tradition and are common not only among Hindus, but also among Sikhs, Jains, Muslims and Christians living in India. The rituals of a wedding can vary widely across the country, but the distinctive feature of a Hindu wedding is the Saptapadi, or Seven Steps in which the bride and groom walk around a blazing fire seven times. Despite the presence of family, friends, relatives, and well-wishers, Hindus recognize that the ultimate witness to the union of man and woman in holy matrimony is the fire god Agni.[26]

As the embodiment of fire, Agni is an important Vedic deity. He is said to be the messenger between humans and gods and delivers the

---

[26] The Sanskrit term *agnisakshi* meaning "with fire as witness" is often used for these occasions.

Agni, the god of fire, riding a ram in an undated Thiruchirappalli painting

sacrificial offerings to the heavens in the form of smoke. In terms of the number of hymns addressed to him, Agni is second only to Indra, which highlights Agni's importance in the Vedic pantheon.[27] Almost all the books of the Rigveda start by addressing Agni. In fact the first hymn in the Rigveda is addressed to him. Among the Vedic deities, Agni alone posed a serious challenge to Indra's supremacy. His dominance can be

---

[27] Of the 1,028 hymns in the Rigveda, 289 are dedicated to Indra and 218 to Agni.

seen in the fire god of Iranian mythology, which was developed from the same Aryan roots. Agni is said to be the son of Prithvi and Dyaus and therefore the brother of Indra or sometimes even his twin brother. Because of Agni's close association with Indra, Agni took on a mythology that was, in many aspects, similar to that of Indra's.

Agni is said to have been born in a certain form in each of the three regions of the Vedic universe. As a thrice-born deity, he manifests as flames of the sun in the heavens, as lightning in midair, and as altar fire on earth. He comes to life on earth as the product of friction between a male and female stick. Just as a fire stick turns to ashes while trying to sustain a fire, Agni is said to symbolically feed upon his parents, who cannot nourish him after his birth. After he devours his parents, he seeks other sources of sustenance for his survival. Just as Indra draws his strength from soma, Agni feeds on ghee (clarified butter) that has been emptied onto the sacrificial fire.

Agni's earthly life has two aspects. As Jataveda, he is called upon to burn offerings; in this capacity he acts as the sacrificial priest and becomes a messenger between humankind and the gods, delivering the sacrificial offerings that ascend as smoke to the heavens. As a Kravyad (flesh eater), however, Agni is invoked to consume corpses and carrion. Among the Vedic gods he is immortal and sometimes said to be ever youthful, although as the originator of sacrificial rites, he is the oldest of all priests.

Although Agni himself is a consumer of flesh offered at sacrifice, he is blessed with the ability to not only remain pure but also to purify impure objects by consuming them. The Mahabharata gives the reason for this blessing. It says that the sage Bhrigu married a woman who was betrothed to a demon. Fearing reprisal from the demon, the sage carried her off to a secret place. The demon, who knew that as fire Agni had access to all places, enquired the deity about the woman's whereabouts. In his characteristic truthfulness, Agni revealed the location. The demon dashed to the secret location and took the woman to his home, much to the dismay of Bhrigu, who put a curse on Agni that he shall eat everything – both pure and impure. But Agni protested that honesty had always been his standard policy and in speaking the truth he did only what a *deva* should do. Fortunately for Agni, common sense prevailed. Bhrigu relented by turning the curse into a blessing. That is why impure objects consumed by fire become pure.

Like Indra, Agni is relentless in his fight against the demons. He is best known for his tussles with the Kravyads, who were known as flesh-eating *rakshasas* (man-eating demons). Even though Agni himself was a Kravyad in one of his forms, he was summoned by Indra to destroy them. For this purpose Agni assumed his Kravyad form and became an obnoxious monster with tusks. Roaring like a bull, he charged among the Kravyads, piercing them with his sharpened tusks and swallowing them.

Agni is often depicted as a red man who has two heads and three legs. He has seven arms and rides a ram. From his mouth fork seven fiery tongues of flame that lick up the sacrificial butter. He is sometimes known as Sapta Jihva, meaning "one with seven tongues." With the coming of the Brahmanic age, Agni's standing eroded like that of every other Vedic god, but not to the same extent as Indra's reputation (more about this later).

> *The most powerful weapon on earth is the human soul on fire.*
>
> —FERDINAND FOCH, 1851-1929

13

Agni Becomes the Purifier of Fire Sacrifices

If you mention "Agnihotri" in Bollywood, the conversation will inevitably turn to Rati Agnihotri, who became a movie star when she was only sixteen and acted in more than three hundred movies. Outside Bollywood, however, the term *Agnihotri* has for centuries been linked to the family of Brahmin priests who perform fire sacrifices according to Vedic rites. As an Agnihotri, the actress hails from this ancient lineage of priests who conduct rituals for the fire god Agni.

In the later texts of the Rigveda, Agni is no longer the lord of fire and his previously undisclosed parentage is revealed—he is said to be the son of Saptarishi Angiras. Agni has become the king of Pitris, the spirits of the deceased. According to the Vedas, one of the destinations of human souls after death is the Pitri Loka, or the abode of ancestors. (The Pitris are forefathers and their abode is equivalent to heaven. Only the virtuous few are allowed entry to this place.) Originally Angiras was the king of Pitris, but he and Agni agreed to swap duties, and Angiras became the priest of the gods and lord of sacrifices.

Agni is now worshipped less as a fire god and more as a purifier of sacrificial offerings. All solemn rites, such as those of marriage and death, honor his presence. However, like many of his contemporaries, Agni eventually lost the preeminence he enjoyed in the Vedic period. The Mahabharata says that he had become greedy and exhausted his vigor by devouring too many oblations. Agni wanted to recover his lost strength by devouring the whole Khandava forest, but Indra thwarted him for a long time. In the end Agni succeeded with help from Krishna.

Although Agni's chief role nowadays is as the purifier of fire sacrifices, he is often connected with a number of beliefs and practices in Hinduism, one of which is Agni Pariksha, or trial by fire. Often called the litmus test of chastity, this practice became contentious in the Agni Pariksha of Sita, the beloved wife of Rama in the Hindu epic Ramayana in which the demon king Ravana abducts Sita and holds her captive in his kingdom of Lanka. To free his wife Rama invades Lanka with an army of monkeys and slays Ravana. Upon rescuing Sita, Rama has qualms about Sita's purity, for she has been a hostage of Ravana for several years. Rama, the Maryada Purushottam, or the perfect man, as he is often called, arranges an Agni Pariksha to test her chastity despite the protests of many, including his brother Lakshmana. Consequently Sita walks through a pyre of burning flames. Although Sita comes through the fire test unscathed and proves her chastity to everyone, whether Rama was right to demand that his wife participate in an Agni Pariksha is a matter of raging debate even today.

Hindu rituals like *havan* (*homa* in South India), or the more elaborate ones like *yajna* or Agnihotra, involve making offerings to a consecrated fire accompanied by the chanting of mantras (prayers). Since fire is central to all Vedic rituals, another tradition associated with Agni is Agnicayana, or the building of fireplaces, considered one of the sacred of the Vedic rituals. An ancient form of this ritual, called Atiratra Agnicayana, which translates as "the building of fireplace overnight," is performed even today by Brahmin priests. The Nambudiri Brahmin families of Kerala, India, are said to have been conducting this ritual for more than three thousand years without a break in continuity.

The Agni Pariksha of Sita by an unknown artist, ca. 1900

For Hindus Agni dwells in every abode, and they call him the lord of the house. He is considered an immortal, one who has chosen to live among mortals. Hindus pray at home shrines or temples by singing hymns and chanting mantras in his presence. It is not surprising every mantra ends with Svaha, because Svaha is the wife of Agni and is symbolized as a witness during the chanting of mantras. Agni is honored by maintaining fires in a certain direction during rituals. The fire facing east is used for sacrifices to the gods; the one facing south is for sacrifices to the spirits of the dead; and fires that face west are used for cooking.

> *Cooking is one of the strongest ceremonies for life. When recipes are put together, the kitchen is a chemical laboratory involving air, fire, water and the earth. This is what gives value to humans and elevates their spiritual qualities. If you take a frozen box and stick it in the microwave, you become connected to the factory.*
>
> —LAURA ESQUIVEL, 1950-

14

Surya – The Sun God

The rumblings of his vehicle can be heard from afar when he makes his daily appearance in a golden chariot pulled by seven horses. With golden hair and arms, Surya is the chief sun god and can often be seen carrying a lotus in each hand; he frequently appears with his charioteer, Aruna. Golden rays emanate from Surya's body, and his magnificence won admiration and praise from many gods and mortals. Yet no one admired him more deeply than Sanjna, the goddess of clouds and the daughter of Tvashtri (the architect-engineer Vishwakarma). With her father's blessing she walked around a fire seven times while holding hands with Surya and married him.

Their marriage produced three distinguished children, Manu (the Seventh and the present), and the twins Yama and Yami, who became the first man and woman.[28] Every marriage has its ups and downs, and this marriage was no different. As time passed, Sanjna, whose name means understanding, could not bear the brightness of her husband anymore. Reluctant to break his heart, she ran away leaving a handmaiden called

---

[28] Yama later became the king of death.

Chhaya (Shade) in her place. Chhaya was an exact replica of her. Sanjna soon found solace in a forest, where she lived disguised as a mare and devoted herself to religious pursuits.

Surya, the sun god

Such a perfect doppelgänger was Chhaya that Surya never found out about the substitution and sired four more children. In her dual role as mother and stepmother, Chhaya was exemplary for many years, but one day she became annoyed and cursed her stepchild Yama. The curse took effect immediately and aroused the suspicion of Surya. A long-standing feature of Indian curses is that a real mother's curse does not have any impact on her own child. For Surya, who provides light to the world, this was the moment to shine the light inward. Soon Surya came to know that his wife had forsaken him long before, leaving another woman in her place. Through his powers of meditation, he found Sanjna in the forest. Turning himself into a stallion, he approached her for companionship. Their courtship resulted in the birth of twin horsemen called the Ashvins, who later became physicians to the gods.

For some time Surya and Sanjna lived together as horses, but they eventually got tired of forest life. They changed back to humans and decided to return to their own dwelling on the condition that Surya had to reduce his brightness by one-eighth. Because sunglasses had not yet been invented, Surya had no other option. His father-in-law, Vishwakarma, the architect of the gods, placed him in a lathe and shaved his brightness from every part of his body except his feet. From the fragments Vishwakarma forged the weapons of the gods, including the wonder-working discus of Vishnu, the trident of Shiva, the lance of Kartikeya (the god of war), and the weapons of Kubera (the god of riches). It is said that the couple lived happily thereafter.

As a testament to his magnificence, the Vedic Surya riding his chariot pulled by seven horses is depicted in this chapter and on the front cover of this book.

Three things cannot be long hidden: the sun, the moon, and the truth.

—BUDDHA

❂ ❂ ❂

15

The Sunset of Surya

As one of the three supreme deities of the Vedic period, Surya, along with Agni and Vayu, was a member of the earliest Hindu triad. Like Agni and Indra, Surya was considered a son of Dyaus. In Puranic times, however, Surya's parentage was reassigned. After he absorbed the characteristics of the other two sun gods, Savitar and Vivasvat, Surya was described as an Aditya—the son of Aditi, the boundless heaven, and the sage Kashyapa. Sometimes Surya is also described as the son of Brahma and the progenitor of the human race. The Hindu swastika, a symbol of good luck and fortune, has been associated with him since ancient times. His Greek counterpart is Helios, and Sanjna, Surya's wife, is sometimes associated with Demeter, the Greek goddess of agriculture.

Surya, who is also known as Savitar, is sometimes celebrated as a benefactor of humans and a slayer of demons. The gods and demons once clashed after Brahma apportioned all sacrificial offerings to the gods and left nothing for the demons. The demons were displeased and a war ensued. The gods found themselves losing to the demons, who forced the gods to give up their place in heaven and their offerings. Aditi was greatly distressed to see the demons tormenting her sons, so she prayed to Surya for help. Surya then was born as her son—with only a thousandth of his full wattage—and defeated the demons and established righteousness. In another instance a set of terrorizing *rakshasas* called Mahadhas, who had the collective intelligence of a piece of furniture, went on a mission to the sky to attack Surya and devour him, but they became incinerated and died as they approached him.

Surya is said to have many children, both legitimate and illegitimate, as was common during those times. The Ramayana says that the monkey king Sugriva was the son of Surya and Aruni, the female form of Surya's charioteer, Aruna. The story can be traced to the case of a devoted wife called Shilavati, who acquired great power through her austerities. One night, as she was complying with the wishes of her leprous husband, Shilavati carried him on her back to a harlot. A sage happened to meet them on their way and, shocked by the man's lust, put a curse on the husband that he would die before sunrise. Using her powers, Shilavati cast a counter spell that prevented the sun from rising the next day. When the sun did not appear on the horizon at the appointed time, Aruna, the charioteer, decided to use of his free time to watch the *apsaras* dance at Indra's court. Disguised as the beautiful woman Aruni, he went to the court—and caught Indra's attention. The attention turned into attraction, and the monkey king Vali was born of this union. Since Aruna was late getting back for the morning ride, Surya demanded an explanation. When Aruna told him the story, Surya became interested in seeing this beautiful woman. Aruna became Aruni once again, but this time for the sun god, and from this union was born Vali's brother, Sugriva, who later became the chief of the monkey gods. Both Vali and Sugriva play key roles in the epic Ramayana.

In the Hindu epic Mahabharata, the hero Karna was also Surya's son. In this story the sage Durvasa granted Princess Kunti a boon when she was young—that she would be able to summon any god and bear a child by him. Eager to test the boon, Kunti unwittingly tested it on Surya and a child was born. Because she was an unwed mother, Kunti wanted to undo the act but could not. Eventually she decided to abandon the child by placing it in a basket afloat on a river. A charioteer found the child and raised him as his own son; the boy later became Karna.

Panoramic view of the Sun Temple of Konark, Odisha, India

Although only a few hymns are addressed to Surya in the Rigveda, the most sacred of the Vedic mantras—the Gayatri Mantra—is addressed to him. Many temples dedicated to Surya can be found throughout India, including the 13th century Sun Temple at Konark in Odisha, often called the Black Pagoda.[29] The temple is laid out as a chariot pulled by prancing horses that the sun god drives across the heavens. Although Surya receives little attention today, he was once regarded as having the same rank as Vishnu, Shiva, Shakti, and Ganesha. These five deities are worshipped by a group of Brahmin priests known as the Smartas. Surya is also worshipped as the supreme deity by a small group known as the Saura sect.

---

[29] The Sun Temple of Konark is often described as one of the seven wonders of India, along with the Taj Mahal and the Khajuraho monuments.

Among the planets, Surya is known as Ravi. Other notable names for Surya include Bhaskara, Dinakara, Mihira, and Marthanda. Many festivals are dedicated to the sun god in India, and the most widely celebrated is the Makara Sankranti, when devotees thank the sun god for ensuring a good harvest. Chhath is another Hindu festival dedicated to him—and Hindus believe it was started by his son Karna.

The time to repair the roof is when the sun is shining.

—JOHN F. KENNEDY, 1917-1963

❖ ❖ ❖

16

The Sun Temple of Konark

One of the grandest scenes in Hindu mythology is the picture of the Vedic Surya making his daily appearance in a golden chariot pulled by seven horses. A 13th century king attempted to immortalize the legend of the sun god by building a massive temple in the form of a chariot with twelve pairs of stupendously carved wheels. The architecture was so awe-inspiring that seven hundred years later the British historian Percy Brown remarked that if the early Europeans had visited this ancient temple about the same time as Taj Mahal, Konark would have been one of the Seven Wonders of the World—not the Taj Mahal.

Today the Sun Temple of Konark is a UNESCO World Heritage Site. It was built at the mouth of a dried-up river in the coastal city of Konark, in the Indian state of Odisha, formerly known as Orissa. The word *Konark,* which means "angle of the sun" in Sanskrit, is a combination of *kona* (angle) and *arka* (sun). Known for its rich temples, Odisha

Sun Temple of Konark

is home to four of the famous ancient temples of India,[30] yet the Konark Sun Temple is the most impressive and has become the cultural symbol of the state. One of the rare temples dedicated to the sun god, the Konark temple has served as an important landmark for mariners (Odisha is on the Bay of Bengal) and was called the Black Pagoda by European sailors.[31]

The temple is said to have been built by the Ganga ruler Narasimha Deva during his reign (1238–64 CE). The construction of the Konark temple was a revolutionary undertaking at that time, not only for its

---

[30] The four temples are dedicated to the four main deities: Konark to Surya, Jajpur to Durga, Bhubaneswar to Siva, and Jagannath Puri to Vishnu. The other important Surya temples are at Martand (Kashmir) and Modhera (Gujarat). Most temples in India were built to honor these widely worshipped deities: Shiva, Shakti, Vishnu, Ganesha, and Muruga.

[31] The Jagannath temple at Puri in Odisha was called the White Pagoda.

sheer scale but because the Surya cult had nearly died out in 13th century Odisha. According to local tradition, construction took twelve years with the assistance of twelve hundred architects, and a workforce of twelve thousand. It was completed in 1258 CE. The number twelve evidently had a special significance for the Surya cult. The sun god has twelve names and the famous Surya Namaskar, or Sun Salutation, has twelve *asanas* (postures).

Chariot wheel with central medallion above an elephant frieze at the Konark temple

Like its counterparts, the Konark temple was built in the traditional style of Kalinga architecture. It was oriented toward the east[32] so that the first rays of sunrise strike the principal entrance. The chariot is drawn by seven horses, which correspond to the days of the week. The twelve pairs of chariot wheels that form part of structure are richly carved and

---

[32] Not all Hindu temples are oriented toward the east. For instance, Angkor Wat, widely considered the greatest of Hindu temples, is oriented toward the west—the direction of Vishnu.

symbolize the twelve months of the year. Each wheel has eight major spokes connected at the center by a medallion carved with images. The wheels rest on a beam that has a frieze carved with figures of elephants, a testament to contribution of elephants to the construction of the temple. More than seventeen hundred elephants appear in various activities, including a scene of catching them in a forest. Assembling the brightest architects of his time, King Narasimha built the massive temple to last an eternity, but it lasted for only about four hundred years. The major tower of the temple, which held the colossal image of *gaja-simha* (a lion on the back of the elephant), crashed in 1628 CE, thereby damaging the image of worship.

You will disappointed to learn that a major part of the temple survives but in ruins. Theories abound for the reason for the collapse. Some suggest that the temple was never completed in the first place or was destroyed when Odisha was invaded by the neighboring ruler Kalapahada. Other theories include weakening of the tower by lightning or an earthquake. The pioneering archaeologist and art historian James Fergusson[33] attributed the collapse to the marshy foundation, whereas Percy Brown thought the temple was not architecturally sound and collapsed as a result. A structural imbalance, attributed to the king's insistence that the architects speed up their work so the temple could be completed on an auspicious day in the 12th year of construction, is believed to be responsible for the collapse. After the twenty-five-story[34] temple fell, it began to disintegrate and worship at the shrine ceased.

Today the Konark temple is a big attraction for tourists. Even in ruins, the exquisite sculptures adorning the outer surfaces of the temple are remarkable. Executed in hard stone, these sculptures are large, vigorous,

---

[33] The same James Fergusson back in 1843 recognized the real importance of the Ajanta cave paintings and the threats to them and asked the East India Company to protect the caves from the ravages of weather and vandals. Book 4 of this series will address the Ajanta Caves in detail.

[34] With the tower, the Sun Temple would have been seventy meters (nearly 230 feet) high, slightly shorter than the Taj Mahal at seventy-three meters (almost 240 feet).

Elaborately carved dancing women in the Sun Temple of Konark

and full of the warmth of life. Creativity has its own landmines and the temple is also known for its erotic sculptures of *maithunas*. These controversial love themes are later additions to Hinduism, which absorbed a good deal of Tantrism, a cult that attributes mystic significance to sex. The erotic sculpture of Konark, like its counterpart at Khajuraho, has invited many famous remarks. Author Michael Edwardes called Konark "the blue movie of the most sophisticated kind." The renowned Indologist Heinrich Zimmer (1890–1943) wrote, "Numerous erotic scenes suggest the sensuous delights enjoyed by the happy occupants of the Sun-God's celestial realm where 'Bhoga is Yoga,' 'delight is religion.'"

For India religion has never been divorced from life, and life is never complete without erotica. The synthesis of the spiritual and the sensual has been the cornerstone of Indian philosophy. Any refinement would only be a withdrawal, a shrinking from reality. Mark Twain was among those who described the Konark temple as "one of the world's wonders." More profound was Rabindranath Tagore when he wrote: "Here the language of stone surpasses the language of man."

17

Vayu – God of Wind

An important deity of the Vedic period, Vayu was a member of the original Hindu triad alongside Surya and Agni.[35] Indra later replaced him in the triad, yet Vayu maintained his position in the Hindu pantheon and survives to the present day. He is the personification of wind or air, for which he is sometimes called Pavan or Vata. Vayu is also associated with *prana,* or breath. When personified as wind, he is tempestuous in nature and rides a chariot drawn by sometimes two, at other times ninety-nine, and occasionally a hundred or even a thousand horses, the number reflecting the intensity of wind—from the gentle morning zephyr to the terrorizing winds of the monsoons.

When personified as *prana,* he sustains life and therefore is an important deity, as this myth explains. The deities of bodily functions once

---

[35] Sometimes the triad of Mitra, Varuna, and Aryaman is considered the most important.

Vayu, the god of wind by an unknown artist, ca. 1800

became engaged in a contest to determine who among them was the greatest. First, the deity of vision left the body and people became blind. Yet life continued on, although in darkness. Next, the deity of hearing withdrew his support. The world appeared to be a silent movie, yet survival continued and some people even prospered.[36] Then the limbs, followed by all the other organs, stopped working. Life continued, even for people with no limbs or who had other handicaps. Finally, Vayu withdrew his support. All bodily functions collapsed and life came to a complete stop.

Vayu is said to be the king of the Gandharvas, who are exceptional singers and dwell in the foothills of Mount Meru. They are also the husbands of the *apsaras*. Although Vayu maintained a cordial relationship with Mount Meru, myth has it that the sage Narada (the gossip monger of Hindu mythology) provoked him to humble the mountain.

---

[36] For example, the compositions of Beethoven after he became deaf and lived in a world of utter silence are generally considered his masterpieces.

As a result Vayu blew at the mountain with storm force, but Garuda, Vishnu's mount, shielded Meru with his wings. After a year of guarding the mountain Garuda took a break. Vayu seized the opportunity and blew harder, breaking the top off the mountain. It fell into the sea, giving birth to the island of Sri Lanka.

Vayu is often described as a handsome man given to wearing perfumes. Yet beneath the fragrance he can be immoral and downright vengeful. His penchant for disrobing women and lifting their skirts is well known. He was married to a daughter of Vishwakarma but is said to have fathered a son, Hanuman, by a monkey mother. In one version of the story Shiva and Parvati transform themselves into monkeys, engage in monkey mischief, and conceive a child. Shiva realizes that the child will be a monkey and asks Vayu to place the fertilized egg in the womb of the female monkey Anjana, who originally was an *apsara* but was turned into a monkey by a curse. In this version of the tale, while Anjana is walking, Vayu, as breeze, lifts her garments up to her waist and places the egg in her womb, as Anjana continues to walk.

This is the origin of the monkey god Hanuman. He is sometimes known as Maruti (son of the wind) or Anjaneya (son of Anjana). As a child Hanuman is said to have mistaken the sun for a piece of fruit and flown up to the sky to eat it. Indra saw him rushing toward heaven and hurled his thunderbolt, Vajra, and scarred Hanuman's cheek as he crashed to earth.[37] When Vayu saw his son lying unconscious, he became infuriated and withdrew air from the universe. To appease Vayu, Hanuman was given superhuman powers.

Bhima, one of the Pandava brothers and a hero of the epic Mahabharata, was another child of Vayu. He was a product of Vayu's union with Kunti, wife of King Pandu. It is said that when Kunti was young, she sincerely served the sage Durvasa, who granted her a boon to have a child by any god she chose. At first Kunti invoked Surya and gave birth to a child, whom she later abandoned. But after she married Pandu, a curse on the king left

---

[37] This is the origin of the name Hanuman. *Hanu* is Sanskrit for cheek.

her childless for a long time. The king became desperate for a child. With Pandu's blessing Kunti used the boon three more times, and one resulted in the birth of Bhima, whose father was Vayu. Both Bhima and Hanuman are often addressed as Vayuputra, which means "son of Vayu."

On another occasion Vayu became enamored with the beauty of King Kushnabha's one hundred daughters and asked them to marry him en masse. When they refused, saying that they would not marry without their father's permission, Vayu became infuriated and gave all of them crooked backs. The king then pleaded with Vayu to marry them, and when Vayu touched them, the daughters became normal again.

Vayu is said to have sprung from the breath of Purusha,[38] the cosmic man. Later texts, however, describe him as a son of Aditi. Vayu is depicted as a white man who carries a white flag in one hand and rides a deer, which symbolizes his swiftness. Just as Mitra is connected with Varuna, Vayu is often associated with Indra. Like Indra, Vayu has a fondness for soma and is often invited to have the first draft because he is the swiftest of the gods. In the Rigveda only one complete hymn is dedicated to Vayu, although two are addressed to Vata. In six hymns Vayu is joined with Indra as Indra-Vayu. Vayu's equivalent in Greek mythology is Aeolus.

Other names of Vayu are Anila and Marut.

> *The stiffest tree is easily cracked, while the bamboo or willow survives by bending with the wind.*
>
> —BRUCE LEE, 1940-1973

❖ ❖ ❖

---

[38] Purusha is a complex concept and will be elaborated later in this book.

18

The Unsolved Mystery of Soma

If the number of hymns dedicated to a deity is a measure of his standing, then Soma is the third most important god of the Vedic era. Only Indra and Agni—who, incidentally, were his enthusiastic supporters—were more significant than Soma. The entire ninth book of the Rigveda contains 114 hymns and is dedicated to a leafless creeper plant from which the intoxicating drink called soma is extracted. Hundreds of years later the identity of the plant is still one of the greatest unsolved mysteries in Hinduism. From the clues in the Rigveda—grows in the mountains, yellow in color, and hangs from branches—a number of plants, including milkweed, rhubarb, fly agaric mushroom, and cannabis (bhang), have been proposed as candidates and rejected. Because of the magical qualities of the drink, Soma became a god to his consumers and is often called the Indian Bacchus. He underwent an extreme makeover in the late Vedic period and became identified with Chandra, the moon god.

The Vedas say that the soma plant grew in the mountains where the Gandharvas lived, and the gods, knowing its magical properties, wanted to have the plant exclusively for themselves. Brahma's wife, Gayatri, took the form of an eagle and tried to fetch soma for the gods, but she was thwarted by the Gandharvas, the custodians of soma. The gods thereafter played a trick on them. Aware that the Gandharvas were susceptible to feminine charm, Vac, the charming goddess of speech, approached them and asked for soma in the most friendliest and flirtatious manner. The Gandharvas could not resist her overtures and allowed her to take soma to the gods.

When soma was first brought to the gods, they started arguing about who should get the first drink. The gods agreed to resolve this by conducting a race. Vayu dazzled everyone and came in first, followed by Indra. But Indra was not known to be a good loser and asked to share the first quaff with Vayu, who agreed. Soon the manufacture of soma from the raw materials obtained from the mountains became a daily ritual. There were three daily pressings of the soma—morning, noon, and night. To avoid squabbles the gods established an order of precedence for partaking of the potion. All the Vedic gods had a share; some, like Indra and Vayu, had a larger share, and others, like Pushan, were satisfied with smaller quantities. Vayu always had top priority, even though Indra was the soma drinker par excellence.

The god Soma soon personified the drink's extraordinary qualities. The god was considered the source of Indra's strength as a warrior against the enemies of the gods. As a deity, Soma is the blood of animals or sap in plants and resides in all living things. He is the inspiration for those who seek him and is considered the god of poets. Soma's popularity reached far-flung places like Persia, where the divine drink became known to Indo-Iranian tribes. Soon sacrifices to Soma began, with the soma juice as the fundamental offering of the Vedic sacrifices. The juice was obtained by pressing the stalks of the plant between stones and then filtering it through wool. After mixing the juice with water and milk, the drink was first offered to the gods. The priests and the sacrificer consumed the remaining portion. The most famous Vedic rituals like Rajasuya (consecration of the king), Ashvamedha (horse sacrifice), and Vajapeya (drink of power) all involved the use of soma.

The ritual use of soma as an intoxicant did not last long. Two key events led to its undoing. Brahma is said to have cursed intoxicants after committing incest with his daughter.[39] Also, the sage Shukra, the guru of demons, blamed intoxicants for unwittingly drinking the ashes of his disciple Kacha in a cup of wine.

---

[39] Details of this story can be found in book 2 of this series.

19

Soma Becomes Chandra, the Moon God

When I admire the wonders of a sunset or the beauty of the moon, my soul expands in the worship of the creator.

—MAHATMA GANDHI, 1869-1948

Toward the end of the Vedic period, the power of the gods no longer came from soma but from sacrifices made by humans. In a mysterious twist the god Soma became identified with the original moon god, Chandra, who was produced during the churning of the milky ocean.[40] The moon was said to be the cup that held the drink soma for the gods. It was now believed that one reason the moon waxed or waned was because the gods were either filling up or drinking down all the soma. Other mythical accounts of Chandra's lineage, however, say

---

[40] The churning of the milky ocean is a pivotal event in Hindu mythology and is elaborated in book 2 of this series.

that he was the son of Varuna, lord of the ocean, from which the moon rises.

Chandra, the moon god (Mewar painting ca.1700)

Legend has it that Chandra was married to the twenty-seven daughters of Daksha. Chandra's wives were the brightest stars in the Vedic sky and formed the lunar asterism. Chandra loved all his wives but was particularly fond of his fourth wife, Rohini. The other wives became jealous and complained to their father about Chandra's favoritism. Daksha put a curse on Chandra that gave him consumption[41] and childlessness. Soon all the daughters, including Rohini, felt sorry for their husband. They

---

[41] Consumption was the olden name for tuberculosis.

went back to their father and asked him to rescind the curse. Daksha was unable to remove the curse completely but he was able to modify it. As a result Chandra suffered from consumption only periodically—for fourteen days at a stretch. The waxing and waning of the moon was now attributed to this curse.

Chandra became fit and healthy during the other two weeks of a month, and he soon proved able to father children. In the Vishnu Purana, Chandra becomes the son of Saptarishi Atri and is appointed the lord of the stars and planets. After performing the Rajasuya sacrifice in which he was consecrated as king, Chandra was able to acquire universal dominion. So much glory, however, went into his head. He became so arrogant and daring that he abducted Tara, the wife of Brihaspati, the advisor of the gods. Although Brihaspati had great occult powers, he was unable to do anything and appealed to Brahma for help. Brahma, however, was unable to persuade Chandra to return Tara, so he turned to Indra for assistance. Chandra and Indra were once partners in the infamous seduction of Gautama's wife, Ahalya. But instead of playing his usual role as seducer of women, Indra became a staunch defender of dharma (divine law) and decided that the only way forward was to take Tara by force. But Chandra had anticipated Indra's move and struck an alliance with the *asuras*. A fierce battle ensued between the gods and the demons with neither side able to score a conclusive win.

Meanwhile Brahma made another appeal to Chandra, and this time Chandra agreed to return Tara, and did so promptly, because he had reached the waning phase of his infatuation with her. But Tara was visibly pregnant, so Brihaspati refused to accept her until after the child was born. To bring this saga to an end, Brahma intervened once again and used his powers to fast track the baby's arrival. When the gods beheld the newborn, they were stunned by its beauty. Both Chandra and Brihaspati immediately claimed to be the child's father. Only Tara knew the identity of the father, but she was reluctant to speak. Finally, after a great deal of coaxing, Tara confessed that the father was indeed Chandra. The child was named Budha, who is not to be confused with Buddha, the founder of Buddhism.

The story does not end there. Having become a step-father while still married to the same woman, Brihaspati was incensed with his wife and cursed her to be reduced to ashes. Brahma, however, felt some sympathy for Tara, and revived her, purifying her in the process. And he successfully persuaded Brihaspati to take her back.

At about the time Chandra abducted Tara, Varuna decided to meet his son. Chandra thought his father wanted to give him advice or perhaps show sympathy to him. Not that long before, Varuna himself had kidnapped the wife of a sage and hid her under the ocean before returning her. Contrary to expectations, Varuna punished Chandra for his behavior by disowning him. But Lakshmi, Chandra's sister, felt sorry for her brother—who had only repeated what his father had done before—and approached Parvati to ask for help from her husband, Shiva. Without any reservations, Shiva forgave Chandra. Shiva also wore the crescent moon on his forehead to show his support for Chandra.[42] At the next assembly of gods, Brihaspati caught sight of Shiva and became annoyed at the half-moon on Shiva's forehead. He protested that Shiva was disrespecting the company of gods by associating with Chandra. A dispute arose between the two, and Brahma had to broker a settlement. Brahma was the ideal judge because he had witnessed all that had happened between them. He declared in favor of Brihaspati. Chandra was thereafter banished to the outer atmosphere and forbidden entry to heaven.

Chandra is most often depicted as sitting in an elaborate chariot drawn by either an antelope or ten white horses. He usually has four hands, one carrying a mace, one carrying soma, another carrying a lotus, and the last offering blessings. He is also a planet in Hindu astrology. Chandra is considered the god of the mind; to appease him Hindus apply a *tilak* (small mark) to their forehead between their eyebrows. Chandra is often said to radiate happiness, and women pray to Chandra for happiness in their married life.

---

[42] Shiva is often referred to as Chandrasekhara, or "the one who has the moon for a crest."

Monday is *somvar* in Hindi and is recognized as the day of Chandra. Hindus believe this is the best day to worship him. Chandra is also considered a fertility god because the dew that falls on plants overnight and sustains them appears to come from the moon. For that reason couples often pray to him when they want a child.

The moon also goes by other names, such as Rajanipati (Lord of Night), Indu (the Bright Drop), and Kshuparaka (One Who Illuminates the Night).

> *Everyone is a moon, and has a dark side which he never shows to anybody.*
>
> —MARK TWAIN, 1835-1910

❂   ❂   ❂

20

An Ancient Civilization That Challenged the Chronology of Hinduism

I've heard that story before, but the version I know had a different ending" is an oft-repeated refrain about mythology. This is true not only of Hindu mythology but of Greek and Roman folklore as well. Why, you may ask? The fact is myths are nested within historical periods and undergo change as they move from one time to another and from one place to another while adapting to the new social context. The myth told in the medieval period of India will differ from the version put forward during the epic period. For instance, Indra did not consult Shiva or Vishnu while drinking soma and preparing for war, as they were not the supreme deities in the early stories of the Aryans. Shiva and Vishnu came to prominence only during later periods.

So which are the key historical periods of Hinduism? Indian culture has many roots, but two of the most important ones are founded in the Indus Valley Civilization and the Vedic culture. Although most scholars agree on the overall classification of the periods, their dates, particularly the dates of the Vedas, are the subject of considerable debate and controversy. For instance, the Vedas were said to have been composed between 1500 BCE and 500 BCE. However, some positions of the stars and planets mentioned in the Vedas could have occurred only between 3500 BCE and 4000 BCE. A similar controversy involves the birth date of Buddha. The Northern Buddhist schools of thought believe Buddha lived around 1000 BCE, but it appears that western scholars have shuffled the dates to about 500 BCE to fit into the theory of Europe as the cradle of civilization. Recent archaeological findings in the Indus Valley speak convincingly for the need to overhaul the chronology of Hinduism, but correcting India's misinterpreted past remains a fluid and controversial enterprise.

A listing of the historical periods of the development of Hinduism is appended below.

Prehistory and Indus Valley Civilization (7000 BCE – 1500 BCE)	
7000 – 5000 BCE	Early agriculture in Indus Valley area
5000 – 2000 BCE	Urban civilization appears along Indus River
1900 – 1500 BCE	Decline of the Indus Valley Civilization

For most of Indian history, until the British arrived in India in the early 17th century, no one disputed the indigenous authorship of Vedic literature. However, when British rule began in earnest in the late 18th century, some British scholars and a prominent German missionary-cum-scholar, Max Müller, who was then living in Britain and benefiting from the subsidies, attributed authorship of the Vedas to the Aryans, who, they claimed, had invaded India sometime around 1500 BCE.

In the 1920s an AWOL British soldier first noticed the Indus Valley ruins at Punjab, where he encountered the remains of the ancient city of Harappa. Further excavations unearthed another major city, Mohenjo-daro, and a number of other sites—which, in turn, led to the discovery of a civilization that was more than 5000 years old and much bigger than that of the Nile Valley in Egypt or the Tigris and Euphrates valleys in Sumer (Iraq). Examination of the ruins revealed that the Indus Valley was well organized and solidly built out of stones and standardized bricks. Large, complex citadels were built on hills and housed palaces, granaries, and public baths.

When a few skeletal remains were uncovered at Mohenjo-daro, they were initially thought to be the skulls of the last inhabitants of the city, thereby validating the British colonial theory that Vedic Aryans had invaded India in hordes from southern Russia and Central Asia. The search for the original homeland of Indo-Europeans was of great interest to scholars because Sanskrit, the language of the Aryans, belonged to the Indo-European family along with Greek and Latin. The sky god of the Vedas, Dyaus Pita, is cognate, for instance, with Zeus of ancient Greece and Jupiter (Dju Pita) of Rome. The Vedic heaven, the world of ancestors, resembles the Germanic Valhalla.

The few skeletons that turned up during a decade of searching, however, did not provide evidence of large-scale attacks. So scholars discounted the Aryan invasion theory. Next they proposed that Aryans had trickled into the Indus Valley from the north, and the theory was renamed the Aryan migration theory. The Harappans possessed a script, which they used to inscribe objects. These inscriptions are usually short and made up of twenty-six characters written mostly in one line. Yet the script is a mystery and no one has been able to decode it. Scholars believe that only a bilingual text, one using the Harappan script against another already known script, would untangle the mystery, in the same way as the decryption of the Rosetta Stone in Egypt, containing the same text in three languages, unraveled the puzzle of hieroglyphs. Since no one has been able to decipher the script, some scholars are questioning whether the inscriptions are indeed a script.

In the 1980s proponents of the migration theory were dealt a major setback. Satellite images of areas in northwest India and in Pakistan revealed the dry bed of a large extinct river. This was the Saraswati River, which the Vedas talk about. The Rigveda placed great importance on the Saraswati, as the book mentions it more than sixty times. Geologists quickly established that the river dried up in 1900 BCE, making the Indus Valley Civilization at least six thousand years old. The newly established link between the Indus Valley Civilization and the Vedic culture then confirmed what Hindus have always believed—the Aryans were indigenous to India. Furthermore, recent archaeological evidence from Indus Valley sites like Lothal, Kalibangan, Surkotada, and Ropar confirms that the sacrificial rites and rituals elaborated in the Vedas are similar to the practices of Indus Valley Civilization. The 19th century Aryan migration theory has now been abandoned, even though a number of scholars steadfastly adhere to the notion of an outside influence.

No one knows why such a remarkable civilization declined and then completely disappeared, although a single major natural disaster, such as a massive flood or a disastrous earthquake, is the prime

The famous Dancing Girl of Mohenjo Daro statuette found in the ruins of Mohenjo Daro in 1926 and believed to be at least 5000 years old

suspect. The Indus Valley is rich in artifacts, but no literary content or paintings (other than pottery) has been found in the ruins, perhaps lost to the ravages of climate and time.[43]

---

[43] Our discussion of the Indus Valley Civilization will be limited in this series, since the subject is discussed at length in *Many Many Many Gods of Hinduism*.

92

21

Yama – God of Death

The life of the dead is placed in the memory of the living.

—MARCUS TULLIUS CICERO, 106-43 BCE

Welcome to the days of our lives. As guests of the planet, you and I share a delightful ride each day in the chariot of time called life. At every dawn we wake up to fulfill our dreams and aspirations. At dusk, we pause for rest and recuperation. We know the wheels of the chariot will stop spinning, and the journey will end one day. But Hindus believe that our journey will continue even after death under the escort of Yama, the god of death.

Who is Yama and why does he carry the designation of lord of death? Yama was a by-product of the love between the sun god Surya and Sanjna before she left him and retreated to the forest. Yama literally means twin, for his sister, Yami, was born at the same time. Together they are considered the first human beings and originators of the human race—and this makes the extremely curious rush to the conclusion that if Yama and Yami are twins and progenitors of the race, their relationship must be incestuous. There was consent but no incest. The Rigveda says that Yami asked her brother to be her husband alluding to the fact that Tvashtri had formed them as man and woman in the womb. But Yama rejected Yami's advances, stating that as lord of the dharma, he would be acting against this very principle.

Yama, the lord of the death, riding a buffalo by an unknown artist, ca. 1800

Yama is often associated with Pluto in Greek mythology. The Rigveda mentions Yama more than fifty times, but only three hymns are dedicated to him. Yama was the first of the mortals to experience death and the first to depart for the Pitri Lok, the world of the ancestors. Hindus consider

Pitri Lok tantamount to heaven, where they are reconciled with their forefathers. Since he had learned how to get to the other world, Yama soon became the tour guide for departed ones, escorting them to the celestial world where they enjoy a blessed life. In the Rigveda, Yama had nothing to do with punishment of the wicked. But, with the coming of the Puranas, the later set of Hindu scriptures, Yama acquired additional responsibilities in his role as the god of death.

It is said that when Yama met a Brahmin girl, Vijaya, he was instantly smitten by her beauty. She was, however, alarmed by his appearance. A fierce-looking man with green skin who wore crimson robes, Yama was a constant reminder of repulsiveness. Coppery eyes stared out of his ghastly face. Riding a water buffalo, he was armed with a heavy mace to strike down his victims and was accompanied by two dogs. As the lord of death, he also carried a noose everywhere and used it to drag his hapless victim to his palace.

Yet something about him piqued Vijaya's curiosity. Yama was a staunch defender of dharma—so much so that he was called the lord of dharma. His cruel-looking exterior hid a compassionate god who always placed dharma ahead of duty. He is known to have exempted some of his victims from certain death and given them another opportunity at life. The Brahmin girl consented to his proposal of marriage even though her brother was vehemently opposed. The beauty and death were soon united in marriage. Shortly thereafter Yama took Vijaya to his abode in Kalichi.

At his place, Yama gave her complete freedom to roam around but cautioned her not to visit the southern portion of his palace. For some time Vijaya abided by the rules, but curiosity got the better of her. She suspected Yama of having a secret wife living in the southern quarters. So she entered the forbidden region, and there, to her utter horror, she saw true hell, with souls trapped in despair. Among the tormented souls she recognized her own mother. Greatly distressed, she went back to Yama and asked him to release her mother. Yama told her that this was possible only through a sacrifice by someone who could then transfer the merit to the poor woman. After some difficulty, a relative was found willing to perform the sacrifice and Vijaya was able to rescue her mother.

In the Puranas Yama is no longer a compassionate figure who welcomes the dead to heaven. At death all souls must now pass before his throne of judgment in Kalichi. His personal accountant, Chitragupta, keeps track of the karmic record of every person during their lifetime on earth. Based on their track record, souls are consigned to the Pitri Loka, to another life on earth, or to one of the twenty-eight torture cells in hell. Yama maintains another book in which he records the span of life allocated to everyone. When a person approaches the end of life, Yama sends his messengers to fetch the person or sometimes rides the buffalo to get the victim himself.

Hindus believe that Yama's messengers, which appear in many fearful forms, arrive to take the dead body to his abode at the hour of death. All souls go directly to Yama at death, and the journey takes four hours and forty minutes. So a dead body should not be burned or cremated until that time has elapsed. Once the time has passed, the process of cremation begins by placing the body on a funeral pyre. Hindus invoke the fire god Agni to convey to Yama that the mortal has been presented to him as an offering.

As Yama is the key decision maker in the journey after life, many have pleaded for mercy after death, some successfully. Others have simply found ways to elude him, such as by invoking any one of the gods of the Hindu triad, as we will see shortly. Vijaya was not Yama's only wife; the best known of his other wives were Sushila and Hemamala. Of his many sons, Yudhishthira, the leader of the Pandavas in the Mahabharata, was the most famous. Both Yama and Yudhishthira are staunch defenders of justice and dharma—which is why both are known as Dharmaraja, or the king of justice. Key epithets for Yama include Dandi (Rod Bearer), Dharmaraja (Lord of Justice), and Mrytu (Death). Yama is the guardian of the south quarter, which Hindus consider inauspicious. They euphemistically refer to death as "going south."

Hindus worship Yama by lighting a lamp, taking a dip in a sacred river, or offering prayers to him at temples. Many also undertake pilgrimages to temples to cleanse themselves of their past sins. Once a year Hindus pay homage to their forefathers through a ritual called Shraaddha.

Nearly all men can stand adversity, but if you want to test a man's character, give him power.

—ABRAHAM LINCOLN, 1809-1865

❁ ❁ ❁

22

Yama Doubles as God of Dharma

> *A million men can tell a woman she is beautiful, but the only time she will listen is when it's said by the man she loves.*
>
> —ZIAD K. ABDELNOUR, 1960-

According to the Mahabharata, Savitri, the beautiful princess and only daughter of a king, fell in love with Satyavan, the son of a hermit, but is warned by sage Narada to cast her love aside, as Satyavan, though unmatched in virtues, is doomed to die within an year. But Savitri is undeterred, for she had already chosen Satyavan as her husband in her mind.

Soon they were married and Savitri, abandoning her royal life, joined her husband and became a forest dweller. Never revealing anything to her husband, she strived hard to forget Narada's words. Nevertheless she performed a series of prayers and penances in the hope that such noble acts will prevent or at least delay his departure from the world. On the fatal day Satyavan set out to cut wood in the forest, but unlike other days he was accompanied by his wife, who walked behind him with a heavy heart. After he chopped a few blocks, Satyavan became dizzy and asked Savitri to support him. She rushed to his side, helped him lie down, and placed his head on her lap. It was then she saw a divine being in blood-red clothes and a crown.

Savitri-Satyavan, painting by Raja Ravi Varma (1848–1906)

Yama announced he was the king of death and had come to take Satyavan. Yama used his noose to force the spirit from Satyavan's body. He then proceeded toward his home in the south with the faithful Savitri in tow. Hearing footsteps behind him, Yama turned around and, on seeing Savitri, asked her to go home and prepare the funeral rites. Yama then continued his south-bound journey, only to realize she was still following him. Once again Yama pressed her to go home, yet after taking a couple of steps, he could still hear her soft footsteps behind him.

Despite his ghastly exterior, the lord of death was a compassionate divine being. Impressed by Savitri's devotion to her husband, Yama granted her a limited boon, one she could ask for anything except the life of her husband. Savitri asked Yama to restore the sight of her father-in-law—which he granted at once. Despite obtaining this, Savitri continued to follow Yama. He granted her two more boons and again tried to dissuade her from following him. But Savitri replied, "If there is any pleasure in this world without my husband, I don't want it. If there is a heaven without my husband, I don't want to be in it. If there are riches waiting for me, I don't want it without my husband. I am as good as dead without him. And as his wife, it is my eternal dharma to follow my husband wherever he goes." Overwhelmed by her words and her matchless devotion, Yama finally granted Savitri an unqualified boon, one with no exceptions. Without a moment's hesitation, she asked to be reunited with her husband. The soul of Satyavan was released, and the couple lived happily thereafter.

The story of Satyavan and Savitri reveals the depth of Savitri's character and her complete surrender in her devotion to her husband. It also shows the compassionate side of Yama for whom occupational duty came second to religious dharma. While Savitri used her true dharma to win over Yama, others have used a variety of ruses to escape the noose, as the following stories describe.

A wicked man called Ajamila spent his entire life flouting dharma with the utmost wickedness. On his deathbed he hollered to his son, who was called Narayana, to bring him a glass of water. Far away, on hearing his name, Vishnu woke up from his famous Ananda Sayana[44] and sent his emissaries to help Ajamila, for the name Narayana is an epithet for Vishnu. When Vishnu's attendants reached Ajamila's house, they found Yama's agents had already assembled there, ready to pluck the spirit from Ajamila's body. A quarrel broke out between the two factions as to who had priority over the matter. Since Vishnu was one of the Trimurti, the triad of three supreme gods, Yama was persuaded to recall his attendants and was deprived of the victim. Ajamila was saved, and this incident changed his life. He became a hermit and practiced austerities to such great effect that he attained liberation when he did die.

In another case Shiva inadvertently rescued a wicked man from the throes of death. A robber by profession, the man was so passionate about his occupation that at his deathbed, he kept muttering words used by thieves—*ahara,* which means "bring the booty," and *prahara,* which means "beat them up." When Yama arrived on schedule to retrieve the soul, he was startled to hear the man say, "Hara, Hara," which is an epithet for Shiva. Yama mistakenly thought the man was invoking Shiva with whom Yama had had a terrible encounter in the past regarding a boy called Markandeya.[45] In a flash Yama mounted his buffalo, made a U-turn, and rushed back to Kalichi. Soon Shiva became aware of what had happened and appeared before the robber. Although the robber had pronounced Shiva's name unwittingly, he was nevertheless granted immunity and given another life as a king. Yes, Shiva is sometimes known to get carried away!

---

[44] Ananda Sayana is the reclining sleep of Vishnu and is mentioned frequently when we describe Vishnu in book 2 of this series.

[45] The story of Markandeya is described in book 5 of this series.

23

How Yami Became
the Lady of Night

Back in the 1980s a California student named Kim West became pregnant by mistake and decided to put the child up for adoption. Immersed in studies, she completely forgot about the child. Thirty years later when she received a letter from her son, Ben, saying that he had been trying to track down his biological parents, Kim was both shocked and overjoyed. The mother and son finally met in 2014, but an incredible thing happened. They fell in love. In fact they were hit by a love so consuming that Ben left his wife and moved in with his mother. The couple say they find each other irresistible because of "genetic sexual attraction" (GSA), a term used for relatives who feel sexual attraction for each other after meeting as adults. "We are like peas in a pod and are meant to be together," said Kim.

You will be mistaken if you think that these things happen only in the United States. Just in the last ten years several family romances have emerged in places like Germany, Canada, and South Africa. An unwelcome phenomenon, GSA raises the familiar topic of taboo: incest.

Although the term was coined by Barbara Gonyo in the 1980s while working with adoptees, GSA is not a recent phenomenon. A version of GSA among twins can be found during Vedic times, in the story of Yami, the twin sister of Yama and the daughter of the sun god Surya and his wife, Sanjna. In Vedic beliefs Yama and Yami are the first mortal humans to be born upon the world.

As twins Yama and Yami were born into a garden of earthly delights. In this natural paradise, time seemed to stand still and it was always day time. The season was always spring, and the sun always shined brightly in the sky. All the creatures lived in peace. In this idyllic setting Yama and Yami lived in harmony with each other. As they grew up, their love for each other blossomed. While Yama had brotherly affection for his sister, Yami sought to unite with her twin brother in an incestuous relationship.

The tenth mandala (book) of the Rigveda contains a hymn that they sing to each other. Yami pleads: "My desire for Yama overwhelms me to lie with him upon the same bed. Let me yield myself to him as a wife would to her husband. Let us roll together like the two wheels of a wagon."

To which Yama replies, "Seek a man other than me and roll together like the two wheels of a wagon. Make your arm a pillow for your consort. Never will I agree to unite my body with your body. They call a man who unites with his sister an evil man. Arrange your pleasures with another, not your brother."

Her overtures shunned, Yami wanders away from her brother, but when she returns she finds Yama lying under a tree; he appears to be fast asleep. She whispers his name, but he does not answer. She calls louder and shakes his body, but Yama does not stir. His body is cold and Yami notices that he is not breathing. Suddenly she is struck with the realization that Yama is no longer alive, and she's completely alone in this world. Yami's grief knows no bounds and tears well up her eyes. Her tears at first become a torrent, then turn into the river Yamuna, which starts to flood the earth. News of the deluge came to the attention of the gods, who became concerned that Yami's mourning would bring about the destruction of the world.

Assuming physical forms, the gods tried to comfort Yami, yet the only words she said were, "But Yama died today! Yama died today!" They tried to console her by telling her that anything born must die one day. They tried to reason with her about the fleeting nature of existence, yet the only words that came from her mouth were "But Yama died today! Yama died today!" Although her love for her brother perpetuated her sorrow, the gods soon realized that Yami was caught in a time bubble. Within the earthly paradise the sun was always shining and it was always "today"—there was no yesterday or tomorrow. The gods reasoned that for Yami's grief to end, they would have to bring today to a close and create an equal interval of night into being.

The gods summoned their powers of creation and first created sunset, so the day would end. This was followed by a blanket of night that enveloped the world. Under the dark skies Yami fell asleep for the first time. While the birds and other creatures were sleeping, the moon and the stars made their first appearance. When the night had passed, the gods created sunrise, causing the sun to rise above the eastern horizon. With the daylight disturbing her sleep, Yami woke up, rubbed her eyes, and said to herself, "Yama died yesterday." The next day the gods heard her say, "Ah, Yama died the day before yesterday."

As the days passed by, the seasons began to make their appearance. With the time bubble burst, Yami experienced less and less grief. As time passed, the soothing balm of night lessened the pain of Yama's death. Although she never forgot her brother, her sorrow lost its power to torment her. Her tears stopped flowing and her sadness became less fiery. The danger she posed to the world slowly dissipated. Yami was the first mortal to experience the true nature of human existence.

After his death Yama assumed the unpopular title of the lord of death. As for Yami, without her radiant brother, she transformed into the goddess Yamini, the mournful woman of the night, and became associated with the moon. In death Yami did not travel to the land of the dead. Instead she became part of nature. Yami gave us the human reset button called night. Hindus in North India unabashedly celebrate the platonic relationship of brother and sister by dedicating to it an entire day of the five-day festival of Diwali, the biggest and brightest of Hindu festivals. Called Bhai Dooj, the occasion marks the last day of Diwali. It is believed that Yama visits his sister every year on this day, and she graces the occasion by placing a *tilak* on his forehead as a symbol of protection.

Although Yama found himself trapped in the land of death, Yami's career took off after the Vedic period. As the goddess Yamuna, she became one of the sacred rivers of India, second only to the Ganges, the holiest of all rivers. She was next associated with Krishna and played an important role in his early life. In later literature she became Kalindi (the Dark One) and eventually one of the wives of Krishna.

❂ ❂ ❂

24

The Paradox of Rudra, the Howler

The scientific types define lightning as a natural electric discharge of very short duration, usually between high-voltage oppositely charged clouds, that is accompanied by a bright flash and sometimes thunder. If you didn't understand that explanation, that's okay. Specialists use jargon that few people outside their field can comprehend. Fortunately there are other ways to describe the phenomenon of lightning. For instance, the Vedic seers saw lightning as the result of the ongoing tussle between heavenly deities that represent the forces of nature and their demonic counterparts. The Rigveda identifies three types of lightning. The one accompanied with little or no rain is commonly associated with the demon Vritra. The lightning followed by a downpour is connected with

Indra. And the maleficent lightning that kills people and causes widespread destruction is attributed to a minor deity called Rudra, who later became one of the eight forms of Shiva. Today Shiva is one of the most popular gods of Hinduism and attracts a group of three hundred million devotees called Shaivites.[46]

As a storm god, Rudra, "the terrible," is a mystery, and scholars and academics, scouring ancient texts, are puzzled by his enigmatic behavior. Known as the howler or the weeping one, Rudra carries many contradictions that people are drawn to him. He can endear yet create fear; he can heal diseases yet spread them like wildfire; he can be calm and collected at one moment yet given to a temper tantrum the next. Only four hymns are dedicated to Rudra in the Rigveda, although it makes more than seventy references to him—about the same as the number of references to Yama. While Yama struck fear with his visage and accoutrements, he was never as menacing as Rudra. In later texts, after Yama was relegated to serving as the god of death, Rudra became more powerful through his association with Shiva.

Rudra has two opposing personalities—terrible and pleasing. As an archer, he always carries a bow. If Indra was famous for his thunderbolt, Rudra was notorious for his bow. When he is being fearsome, Rudra is described as the divine archer who fires at gods, men, and cattle, either killing them outright or infecting them with mortal diseases. Like Shiva, he has an appetite for fierce, unpredictable, destructive deeds. Everyone lives in fear of Rudra, because he is unpredictable. A minor transgression by a faithful devotee can propel Rudra into a tempestuous rage.

When he is pleasing, Rudra is described as young, intelligent, and the most beautiful of the gods. As the greatest physician, Rudra is said to possess hundreds of remedies that he dispenses to his devotees. Since his animal is the bull, Rudra holds the title of Pashupati, or Lord of the Cattle—which is the form in which he is worshipped most often. According to the British academic Robin Zaenher, devotees flock to

---

[46] The followers of Shiva are also known as Shaivas.

Rudra in this form because they see themselves as the herd with Rudra as the leader. The bull is a symbol of both rain and fertility in Vedic culture. That is why he is sometimes referred to as the provider of fertilizing rains.

Unlike Indra, Rudra is not confined to palaces. He is the man of the wild and keeps his residence in the hinterland—like the forest or mountains. In myths Rudra epitomizes many of the vital qualities of Varuna and is often invoked for protection against the decrees of Varuna. One key attribute of Varuna, his supernatural power, or *maya,* seems to have gradually become Shakti, the creative force identified as the supreme power of Rudra (and Shiva). Whereas Varuna inspired awe and fear in pre-Vedic times, Rudra (and later Shiva) created the same intensity of opposing feelings in later times.

Rudra is officially acknowledged as the father of a group of storm gods called Maruts, who are said to have been born from the laughter of lightning. Also known as Rudriyas (sons of Rudra), the Maruts were the constant companions of Indra in his battle against the demons. Rudra and his sons are known to wear ornaments of gold and are armed with weapons like the bow and arrow, although Rudra by himself was never associated with the warlike exploits of the Maruts.

A story about Rudra's name describes him as the son of Ushas, the goddess of dawn, and Prajapati. One day his father found him weeping and asked why the boy was upset. Rudra replied that he wept because his evil had not been taken away. His father named him Rudra, the weeper. He wept seven more times and gained seven other names. These seven names, along with Rudra, became the genesis for the multiple attributes in the manifestation of Shiva. In the eightfold concept of Shiva (known as Ashtamurti among Shaivites), Rudra is one of the attributes of Shiva—not as the terrible god but as the one who dispels sorrow.

From Rudra we get the term *Rudraksha*, which translates as "Rudra's eyes" and refers to the Rudraksha tree or its brown seed. Evergreen and broad-leaved, the Rudraksha tree grows in the hilly regions of the Himalayas and other parts of the world, including Southeast Asia and Australia. The seeds of the Rudraksha tree are unique in that each seed has a natural hole in the middle, making them easy to string together as beads for a necklace or rosary. This has made them popular for creating organic jewelry, or *mala*.[47] Legend has it that Rudraksha beads are the tears of Shiva after he decimated a triad of demons called Tripurasura, who were devoted to him.

Rudraksha beads

In mythology Tripurasura is a collective name given to the three sons of the demon Taraka.[48] Many versions of this story exist, but one version says that Tripurasura performed severe austerities in their quest for power and obtained a boon from Brahma. Because their father was killed by Shiva's son Kartikeya, the demon trio asked for immortality. But Brahma flatly refused their request, saying it was against the dictates of dharma. Tripurasura then asked to be blessed with impregnable fortresses in three different cities that can be destroyed only by a single arrow—which they knew only Shiva could do. Brahma granted their request, although he knew he might regret his magnanimity. The demons,

---

[47] Rudraksha mala is a necklace usually strung together from 108 beads and used by Hindus and Buddhists as an aid in counting while they are chanting mantras.

[48] The mythology of Taraka and his annihilation by Shiva's son Kartikeya appears in book 5 of this series.

however, thought that so long as they were devotees of Shiva, they were assured of immortality.

Three magnificent cities (known as Tripura, which means "three cities") and the fortresses were built at three separate locations by the demons' own architect, Mayasura, who also was a devotee of Shiva. These towers of power were located on earth, in the sky, and heaven and had walls of iron, silver, and gold, respectively. The locations were chosen in such a way that cities aligned in a single line only once every one thousand years. The Tripurasura were thus assured of the safety of their fortresses. Soon other demons began to flock to the newly created cities, which offered prosperity and peace.

After several years of peace and harmony, the evil tendencies of the *asuras* resurfaced. As they became steeped in luxury and power, the *asuras* forgot their devotion to Shiva. Safe behind the impregnable forts, they embarked on a spree of terror, waging wars without provocation and lashing out at mortals and *devas* (demigods). Soon Indra and the gods approached Shiva for relief from the rampaging demons. Shiva told them that he would transfer half his strength to the gods, which would allow them to overcome their enemies. But the gods could not support half of Shiva's strength, so instead they gave half of their own strength to Shiva. Meanwhile a magnificent chariot of gold along with weaponry was built by the god's architect Vishwakarma for the military operation. Shiva braced for battle but had to wait a thousand years for the three fortresses to line up. When the moment arrived, Shiva used the mighty Mount Meru as his bow, strung a single arrow with Vishnu as its shaft and Agni at its tip, and let it fly. The arrow pierced the three forts at the same time and engulfed them in flames. The only demon to survive was Mayasura.

The death of his devotees caused Shiva to shed some tears—which became Rudraksha beads. Shiva also became more powerful because of the strength obtained from other gods, an oft-cited reason for his prowess. As for Rudra, despite the awe and fear he generated in his heyday, he is no longer worshipped and has fallen into obscurity. Scholars believe that the many facets to Rudra's character could have arisen from the assimilation of many Vedic gods. The antithetical traits, according to them, are perhaps a consequence of amalgamation of regional and tribal gods that took place under his name, and were later attributed to Shiva. Although Rudra represents a phase in the evolution of Shiva, the worship of Rudra also represents perhaps one of the earliest instances of worship of the power of destruction.

25

Ushas – The Charming Goddess of Dawn

Every day at dawn, before the sun's orb becomes visible, Ushas puts on her embroidered garments. After adorning herself in splendid red veils and gold jewelry, she begins her daily journey on a hundred chariots led by ruddy cows or horses. Opening her blouse to reveal her bosom, she creates light for the world and stirs all creatures from their sleep. From afar the sun watches the young maiden with interest. Enchanted by her appearance, he follows her, and their aerial romance makes the birds chatter and streams gurgle. Soon they are locked in a fierce embrace, but she perishes in the encounter, only to be reunited with her lover the next day.

Celebrated in twenty hymns, Ushas, the goddess of dawn, is mentioned more than three hundred times in the Rigveda. Among the Vedic deities, she's the only goddess of importance. Just as Agni is known for his priestly knowledge, Varuna for his righteous order, and Indra for his strength, Ushas is characterized by her feminine charm. She's been described as the most graceful creation of the Vedic poetry and has inspired some of the most beautiful hymns. A maiden of unsurpassed beauty, Ushas naturally attracted a long list of heavenly lovers, including Surya, Agni, Pushan,[49] and the Ashvins.

As the daughter of Dyaus and Prithvi, Ushas arrives every day without fail. She is a path maker and leads Surya on his journey from the east so that his brilliance and fire are revealed to the world. With her arrival she also drives away her counterpart, the dark oppressive night, or Ratri. As the personification of night, Ratri is the sister of Ushas and is identified with darkness. By removing the black robe of night, Ushas vanquishes bad dreams and wards off evil spirits. She is sometimes referred to as the mistress of time. Although she is the immortal maiden of time who never ages, her daily travels across the morning sky are a reminder to mortals about their limited time on earth.

When the red gleams of sunrise are likened to cattle, Ushas is called the mother of cows. Like a cow that yields her udder for the nourishment of others, Ushas bares her breasts to provide light for the benefit of all creatures. As the regularly recurring dawn, she is associated with Rta and participates in cosmic order. She wakes people up to perform their religious sacrifices in honor of the gods. She also persuades the gods to drink the exhilarating soma and helps to kindle sacrificial fires. For this reason the gods are described as waking with Ushas. Since she precedes the gods of light (Agni, Surya, Savitar, and others), she is called the mother of gods.

The Ushas of the Vedas is identical to the Usha of Avesta, Eos of Greece, and Aurora of Rome. Although she has many epithets—Goddess of Dawn, Mother of Cows, Mother of Gods—she was forgotten in later years despite her importance in the Rigveda. The goddess Aditi has taken over her position and is known as the mother of gods. Yet Ushas is still remembered in contemporary India. She is acknowledged and worshipped in the early hours of dawn during the chanting of Gayatri Mantra.

---

[49] Pushan, the god of meetings, is a Vedic solar deity and one of the Adityas. Ten hymns in the Vedas are dedicated to Pushan.

> *Death is not extinguishing the light; it is only putting out the lamp because the dawn has come.*
>
> –RABINDRANATH TAGORE, 1861-1941

26

How Kubera Became
the God of Wealth

*Don't promise when you're happy, don't reply when you're angry,
and don't decide when you're sad.*

—ZIAD K. ABDELNOUR, 1960-

Throw a lucky man into the sea and he will come up with a fish in his
mouth," says an ancient Arab proverb. In Vedic times this lucky man
was undoubtedly Kubera. Associated with creatures of evil and stealth,
Kubera rose from a small-time crook to become the god of wealth in one
of the greatest stories of divine serendipity.

Originally a part-time robber, Kubera wasn't good at his job even after
years of field experience. He botched many operations so badly that the
victims often handed over the loot out of sympathy. Legend has it that
Kubera once went to rob a temple of Shiva and the wind blew out his
candle. Kubera was so afraid that Shiva might be watching him that his
hands and body started trembling. There aren't too many places to hide

117

when you are in Shiva's crosshairs. With his shaking hands, Kubera tried to light the candle nine times—and failed. In his tenth attempt, he not only succeeded in lighting the candle, but earned so much admiration from Shiva that the bumbling thief was promoted to the status of a god. Both Shiva and Vishnu have been known to occasionally throw the god lottery open to the unsuspecting. They are also known to be extremely loyal to their devotees. It is safe to assume that the last thing on Kubera's mind during the heist was devotion. But Shiva spent his early years as lord of the robbers and is said to have a soft spot for crooks and thieves. They formed an instant friendship, and Kubera became a lifelong buddy of Shiva.

Wall carving of Kubera, the god of wealth

Or maybe Shiva was moved by Kubera's dreadful appearance. Kubera was born deformed, unusually short with three stubby legs supporting a plump body. He had only eight teeth and one eye, having lost his other

118

eye for gawking at Shiva and Parvati at another time. He is often depicted as carrying a money box and a club. Since his mobility was limited, Brahma took pity on Kubera and ordered Vishwakarma, the architect of the gods, to build him a vehicle so he could get around better. The aerial chariot called Pushpaka, which could move of its own accord and was large enough to transport a whole city, was built for Kubera. The flying chariot became a marvelous contraption and a popular mode of transportation among the gods and demons. After Rama defeated the demon Ravana, as described in the epic Ramayana, Rama is said to have used Pushpaka to move him and Sita, along with an entire army of monkeys, back to his kingdom.

But before his encounter with Rama, Ravana had stolen Kubera's chariot and used it as a getaway vehicle when he abducted Sita. Ravana then used the chariot to make aerial attacks on the gods. Because the title of the chariot had Kubera's name, Kubera was blamed for the attacks. Given his dubious reputation, Kubera had to work doubly hard to clear his name. That was not the only time Ravana, his stepbrother, gave him problems. Ravana had also stolen Kubera's palace in Lanka—which Vishwakarma had originally built for the *rakshasas*. The story goes back to the time when the *rakshasas,* anticipating an attack from Vishnu, deserted the city even though Lanka was the richest and best-fortified city at that time. With no one in charge, Kubera took over the ghost city and settled down with his own attendants. A change of circumstances led to enemies becoming friends. When Vishnu was pacified, the *rakshasas* wanted to reoccupy the city. When they learned that Kubera was the king, they sent a beautiful maiden to seduce Kubera's father. She succeeded on multiple occasions, and from their union were born Ravana and three others. By performing austerities Ravana was able to obtain the boon of near-invincibility from Brahma. Ravana then overthrew Kubera and retook the city of Lanka for his people, the *rakshasas*.

After the loss of Lanka, Kubera approached Vishwakarma once again for palatial accommodation. Vishwakarma built him a palace near Mount Kailash in the Himalayas, where Kubera could be close to his good friend

Shiva. In his elevated capacity as god of wealth, Kubera became the over-lord of numerous semi-divine species and the owner of the treasures of the world. He was also appointed as the regent of the north. The magical chariot was returned to Kubera after the defeat of Ravana and became his private jet—which he now uses to shower jewels and other treasures.

The god of wealth also owns Alaka, the richest city in the universe. On Mount Mandara he owns a grove of enormous beauty called Chaitraratha, where the charming lake Nalini is located. According to myth, both Alaka and Mount Mandara are in the Himalayas. Thus Kubera's domains are in the high Himalayas since he is the guardian of the north and the mountains are the repositories of mineral wealth. He oversees the earth's storehouse of treasures, assisted by attendants called Kinnaras, or Indian centaurs.

Pride often causes people to flaunt their wealth and power, and Kubera was no exception. Kubera once decided to host an extravagant feast for the gods to show off his wealth. He invited his good old friend Shiva and other gods. Shiva did not accept the invitation but sent his son Ganesha. The pot-bellied Ganesha arrived with an enormous appetite and started gorging on the food meant for other guests. Kubera ordered his army of chefs to prepare more food, but they could not keep up with Ganesha's gluttony. When Ganesha demanded more food still, Kubera realized this was not a case of real hunger. He headed to Shiva's abode and groveled at his feet, apologizing profusely for showing off his wealth. Shiva accepted his apology and offered the rampaging Ganesha a few stems of durva[50] (Bermuda) grass, which instantly quelled his appetite.

Although Kubera had driven the bar for acceptable heavenly behavior below sea level, he is worshipped in India as the treasurer of the riches of the world. His role, however, has been taken over by Ganesha, the obstacle remover and the god of wisdom and fortune, with whom Kubera is

---

[50] While the most sacred herb in India is *tulsi* (basil), the second most sacred is durva, or Bermuda grass, which is often regarded as a noxious weed in other countries. In Hinduism *tulsi* is sacred to Krishna and durva is sacred to Ganesha.

often associated. Like Ganesha, Kubera is also worshipped outside India, particularly in Thailand. Kubera is also a leading figure in Buddhist and Jain mythology.

Kubera is also inextricably linked to the Venkateswara temple of Tirupati, one of the most popular places of worship in the world. Legend has it that Vishnu fell in love with a young local woman and offered to marry her, but the girl's father demanded a large dowry. To finance the deal Vishnu took a large loan from Kubera, who stipulated in the prenuptial agreement that Vishnu could return to his celestial home at Vaikuntha only after he repaid the loan. Today devotees visiting the temple always offer money to help Vishnu repay his debt. Not surprisingly, the Venkateswara temple in Andhra Pradesh is the richest temple in India in terms of donations received.

It's hard to detect good luck—it looks so much like something you've earned.

—FRANK A. CLARK, 1860-1936

❖ ❖ ❖

27

Kama – God of Love

Once difficult to access because of rough terrain, the temples of Khajuraho are now a UNESCO World Heritage Site and are visited by hundreds of thousands of tourists every year. Among the many intricately carved statues, a few panels with erotic themes have attracted worldwide attention. These reliefs enshrine the spirit of love and have been called the *Kama Sutra* in stone. Although the word *kama* originally referred to the sensuous pleasure derived from the aesthetic enjoyment of life, it has taken on an unmistakable connotation of sexual desire, which Hindus believe is the work of Kamadeva, or simply Kama, the god of love.

Kama, the god of love, in what is believed to be an 18th century painting

What Eros is to Greeks or Cupid is to Romans, Kama is to Hindus. Among the gods of the Hindu pantheon, he is the most handsome. Often depicted as an ever-youthful man, he wields a bow and arrow and rides a parrot. The bow is made of sugarcane and strung with a line of humming bees, and the arrows are tipped with fragrant flowers to excite every sense. He is ably assisted by his wife, Rati, and his friend Vasanta, who strings the bow and picks the floral arrow for the chosen victim. As lord of the *apsaras,* Kama is surrounded by these beautiful nymphs, one of whom carries the red banner that bears the emblem of the monster fish Makara, Varuna's mode of transportation.

For Buddha desire was the root of miseries,[51] but for Kama it was the key to the delights of life. Kama loves to roam around and amuse himself by instilling passion in everyone, especially innocent young girls, married women, and ascetic sages. Spring is the season of his revelry when trees bloom and sweet-scented flowers of all colors blossom. He is frivolous in the use of his powers. Wounded by his shafts of desire, wives become adulterous, young women yield to passion, and men commit mistakes. Even *rishis* (Hindu sages) on a stringent regimen of austerities are known to give up asceticism at times and enjoy the warmth of women.

Kama is an ancient god who is discussed in the Vedas, where he manifested as the creative spirit that filled Purusha[52] at the beginning of time. There are two versions of Kama's birth. According to the Mahabharata, Kama was the son of Dharma.[53] The Puranas have a different account of his birth: Brahma first created ten Prajapatis (progenitors), followed by a woman of exceptional beauty called Shatarupa. While Brahma and the Prajapatis were attracted by her beauty, a handsome young man holding a bow and flower-tipped arrows in his quiver sprang from Brahma's mind and looked at him for instructions. Brahma told him to romantically charge all creatures with desire. Without any hesitation, Kama let loose a shaft at Brahma himself which charged him fully, giving an extra boost to his creative prowess.

The shaft of desire, however, led to unintended consequences. After he was struck by Kama's arrow, Brahma fell in love with his own mind-born daughter, Shatarupa, which caused him to commit incest and subsequently lose one of his heads. For Kama's transgression Brahma put a curse on Kama that he would one day be turned into ashes.

---

[51] In the Four Noble Truths of Buddhism, suffering is said to arise from attachment to desires.

[52] Purusha is described later in this book.

[53] Dharma was the ancient name for Yama, who is still known as Dharmaraja. Dharma took off as a new god in Puranic times.

Brahma's words came true, as Kama became a victim of Shiva's wrath. At the time a demon called Taraka was tormenting the gods after receiving a boon from Brahma. The gods wanted to destroy Taraka, but the boon said only a scion of Shiva could do Taraka in. Meanwhile, Shiva was in deep grief over the death of his wife, Sati, and turned himself into an ascetic. As Shiva became numb to emotions, Indra tried to convince Kama to approach Shiva and plant the seeds of desire in his heart. After much persuasion Kama took the risk of shooting his love-laden arrow at Shiva, who became furious at having his meditation interrupted. Shiva opened his third eye and the ensuing flames reduced Kama to ashes.

But the shaft of Kama created an indelible mark on Shiva, for he could not bear the passion that the arrow aroused in him. So he headed to the cooler shades of a forest, but far from getting relief, he was distracted by the sight of the wives of hermits who were living in the forest. He then dipped himself in cold water, but the heat of passion started to boil the water. Eventually Shiva found comfort but only after he married Parvati (who would become Ganesha's mother).

The death of Kama became a big problem. Devoid of love, the earth became barren and infertile. The gods asked Shiva to bring Kama back to life. Kama's wife, Rati, was overcome with grief. She prayed to Parvati, who interceded with Shiva to resurrect Kama. A blueprint was created for Kama's reentry to the world. According to this plan, the god of love would be born as Pradyumna, son of Krishna and Rukmini, and Rati would live in the house of the demon Sambara as Mayavati, the cook. This was a fitting rebirth for the god of love, as Krishna was a renowned master of erotic love.

As soon as Pradyumna was born, Sambara snatched him from his crib and threw him into the sea. The demon had been warned that the child would one day murder him. The baby was swallowed by a fish that was then caught by a fisherman. Sambara unknowingly bought the fish at the market. That night, when Mayavati gutted the fish while preparing dinner, she found the child. As she stood in the kitchen stunned, she had a vision of the sage Narada, who told her that the baby was her husband,

Kama. Narada then gave her special powers that allowed her to make the boy invisible so that she could raise him in secret.

When Pradyumna came of age, Mayavati tried to seduce him, but he protested. Mayavati then revealed to Pradyumna their true antecedents. They became lovers, and subsequently Mayavati became pregnant. It was about time for the couple to return to heaven. When Sambara mistreated Mayavati, Pradyumna flew into a rage and killed Sambara with a single blow. With their respective missions accomplished, the couple then headed to heaven to the abode of Krishna and Rukmini, where Narada told them that they were none other than Kama and Rati, united again.

Multicultural friends celebrating Holi

By now you and I would concur that Kama's resurrection is not the most exciting story in Hindu mythology. Although Kama is not worshipped to the same extent as the other gods, he remains a colorful character and continues to influence human lives. Inspired by Kama, the sage Vatsyayana wrote the treatise *Kama Sutra,* which is widely considered the standard work on love in the Sanskrit literature. The spring festival of Holi,[54] also known as the Festival of Colors, or sometimes as the Festival of Love, is said to commemorate, among many other things, the return of Kama. It is an ancient Hindu festival that has become popular among non-Hindus as well.

While Shiva is proof of the supremacy of asceticism, Kama is proof of the power of eroticism. In religious worship *vibhuti* (sacred ash) is often smeared on the forehead to symbolize victory over desires, a reference to Shiva's battle with Kama. It is true that Shiva reduced Kama to ashes and smeared his own body with the ashes. But Kama rose from his ashes and conquered Shiva. Kama and Shiva therefore share an intimate relationship, and the story of Kama reveals their true interconnectedness.

---

[54] Holi is also celebrated to commemorate Radha's love for Krishna—which is explained at length in book 4 of this series.

28

Vedic Dikpalas – The Regents of Directions

Popularized by the late British cosmologist Steven Hawking, the turtles-all-the-way-down metaphor comes from the ancient, flat-earth theory, which postulates that earth is supported on the back of a world turtle. Who supports this turtle? Another turtle, which, in turn, is supported by yet another turtle leading to turtles all the way down. Like the chicken-and-egg conundrum, the turtles-all-the-way-down metaphor emphasized the idea of endless continuation and is often used when an argument is circular.

Back in the 17th century, it was mistakenly believed that this myth came from India even though variations of the flat earth theory were popular in many cultures including the Chinese. In some of these tales, the turtle was replaced by an elephant or a serpent. Fascinated with world turtles and elephants, the British philosopher John Locke in 1689 claimed—with no supporting evidence—that the Hindus believed the earth is held in the universe by eight pairs of elephants that rest on the back of a turtle. The earthquakes that wreak havoc on earth were caused by elephants and turtle getting tired and shaking their burden. This belief gained currency in the 20th century and was perpetuated by writers like Bertrand Russell and Henry David Thoreau. Although Locke based his claim on hearsay, the turtle-earth myth probably was influenced by the concept of Lokpalas and Dikpalas in Hinduism.

An 1876 drawing of the world supported on elephants, all on the back of a turtle

Meaning "rulers of directions," the Dikpalas are eight in number and rule the eight directions of the universe. In Hinduism each direction is assigned to a deity, who presides over it and is responsible for protecting the occupants. Elephants play a big role in Hindu mythology. They are the mounts of choice for these guardians of directions, and the pachyderms are often accompanied by their mates. Thus Indra rides the elephant Airavata, whose mate is the elephant Abhramu. When the eight gods are depicted in royal attire with their mounts (eight elephants and their mates), the gods are known as Lokpalas, or "rulers of the world." Most of the prominent Vedic gods like Indra, Varuna, Yama, and Vayu are on the list of Lokpalas.

Also on it is the little-known Nirrti, who is often associated with pain, misfortune, and destruction. The Rigveda mentions only one hymn about Nirrti, although she is mentioned several times in the hymn.

Deity	Direction
Indra	east
Varuna	west
Kubera	north
Yama	south
Agni	southeast
Isana (aspect of Shiva)	northeast
Nirrti	southwest
Vayu	northwest

The concept of Dikpalas did not exist in Vedic times. The Rigvedic hymns make no mention of the Dikpalas. During the Vedic period the twelve Adityas—who included luminaries like Indra and Varuna—ruled the skies and watched over the world.[55] Like the Adityas, whose number progressed from seven in the Rigveda to twelve in the Puranas, the Dikpalas also evolved over time. In the Upanishads there were four of them, but by the time of Puranas there were eight.

Even the members of the Dikpalas have changed over time. In the Upanishads Surya was the regent for east, Yama for south, Varuna for west, and Soma for north. Later Indra replaced Surya as the guardian of east. The tantric tradition adopts a three-dimensional view of the cosmos and adds a zenith and nadir, which extends the number of Dikpalas to ten. The two additional regents mentioned in the Tantras are rooted in the myth about Linga of Light[56] in which Shiva appears as the axis of the

---

[55] The twelve Adityas are sun gods, and each Aditya is said to shine during one month of the year.

[56] Shiva and the Linga of Light are discussed in book 5 of this series.

universe with Brahma at the peak and Vishnu at the base.

The significance of the directions and their presiding deities is evident in ancient sacred architecture, particularly in the design of temples and Vedic altars. Their influence also shows up in city planning and ritual offerings. South has been always associated with Yama, the lord of death. Hindus always face south to make ritual offerings to the deceased. The east is the direction for most rituals and ceremonies conducted at home, such as the house-warming ceremony. In some rituals, such as the child-naming ceremony known as *namakarana,* invocations are made to all directions.

The concept of the Dikpalas inevitably associated several deities with one specific direction. It also led to the creation of a number of myths and became the basis for Vastu Shastra, the traditional Hindu system of architecture. Often equated with Feng Shui, Vastu Shastra integrates architecture with nature and is rooted in traditional Hindu beliefs. Originally Vastu Shastra was applied in the architecture of Hindu temples and stipulated the orientation of a temple. Shiva temples, for instance, often face northeast, the direction of Isana, an aspect of Shiva. Vishnu temples face west, the direction of Varuna, an Aditya. The best example of a Vishnu temple is the world-famous temple Angkor Wat[57] in Cambodia, which is oriented to the west. Surya temples, on the other hand, always face east, like the Sun Temple of Konark.

Today the influence of Vastu Shastra can be seen in India as the concepts are applied to both residential and commercial constructions. Such is the popularity of Vastu that the number of Vastu experts is second only to that of cricket, a sport that preoccupies the nation. Furthermore, among the Vastu experts, there are varying opinions on which rules and principles comply with Vastu. Many traditional Hindus believe that the northeastern corner of a room should be left vacant because the direction belongs to Shiva. They would also rather do business while facing north, because Kubera, the lord of wealth, rules the north. Many orthodox

---

[57] Angkor Wat is described in detail in book 2 of this collection.

Hindus also avoid dwellings that face south because it is in the direction of Yama. What if you are stuck with a piece of land facing south? Vastu provides several remedies, such as shifting the main entrance toward the east or making the walls of the south and west higher than those of east and north.

With the increasing pressure of availability of space in modern cities, most people find it challenging to acquire the perfect plot let alone adhere to the Vastu principles. For most households Vastu serves as useful guidelines, not hard-and-fast rules. In short, although the Dikpalas have their own preferred directions, they are not set on stone and can be negotiated or remediated.

❀ ❀ ❀

29

Changes in Religious Beliefs during the Vedic Age

Earlier we alluded to the notion that Indian culture has two important roots, namely, the Indus Valley Civilization and Vedic culture. Having described the Indus Valley Civilization in an earlier chapter, we now take a closer look at Vedic culture.[58]

While the Indus Valley Civilization was rife with artifacts, the Vedic culture was strangely lacking in them. But what the Vedic culture lacked was compensated by the richness of its literary works, such as the Vedas and Upanishads. The actual dates of composition of the Vedas are still a matter of great contention across countries and continents. The pioneering Indologist Max Muller wrote, "Whether the Vedic hymns were composed [in] 1500 or 15000 BCE, no power on earth will ever determine." Muller came to that conclusion because the Vedas were transmitted orally for thousands of years before they were written down. In ancient

---

[58] Our discussion of Vedic culture will be limited in this book since the topic is discussed in detail in *Many Many Many Gods of Hinduism.*

times, writing down the text was considered an act of desecration.

What are the Vedas, you may ask? Although the Vedas contain many books, they can be broadly described as books of hymns called Samhitas and their appendixes. The entire corpus of Vedas consists of four Samhitas (Rigveda, Yajurveda, Samaveda, and Atharvaveda) and three special compendiums of commentaries (Brahmanas, Aranyakas, and Upanishads). The most important of these books is the Rigveda Samhita, a collection of 1,028 hymns containing mostly praises of the Vedic gods (Indra, Agni, Soma, Varuna, and others) or the foundation myths, such as the birth of the world and primordial sacrifice. These hymns were arranged in ten books of unequal sizes called mandalas. When most people refer to the Vedas, they actually mean the hymns section of the collections. The Rigveda Samhita is also the basis of myths discussed in this volume. When were the hymns composed? Although the actual dates of composition cannot be determined with any certainty, scholars believe parts of the Vedas were composed during a span of more than one thousand years. A breakdown of the Vedic period appears in the figure that follows.

Vedic Period	1500 BCE – 500 BCE
Samhita Period	1500 BCE – 900 BCE
Brahmanic and Aranyaka Period	900 BCE – 600 BCE
Upanishad Period	900 BCE – 500 BCE

The caste system first evolved during the Brahmanic age, as a means of integrating people into the social framework. Vedic society was divided into four classes, or castes (*varnas*), based on people's occupations. According to this structure, the Brahmin caste, consisting of priests, was entrusted with the administration of the sacred. The Kshatriyas, which included kings, military nobility, and warriors, were assigned to defend and safeguard society. The Vaishyas were mostly cattle breeders, farmers, and merchants and were responsible for production. The fourth caste, which was considered inferior and excluded from rites, was called

Shudras, and people belonging to this caste worked as servants. Beyond the four castes were outcastes, who undertook the menial tasks that polluted the individual. Only members of the three upper castes[59] could be called Aryans and were considered twice born.

While the Samhitas professed glory to the gods, the mythological landscape changed between the period of Samhitas and that of the Brahmanas. The Brahmanas were mostly concerned with ritual and its effectiveness. Indra was the powerful god during the Samhitas, but during the Brahmanas the role of Agni increased and the symbolism of fire sacrifice became more significant. The Brahmanas[60] even stipulated that sacrifice is effective only if the ritual is observed down to its smallest detail. Thus sacrifice became an end in itself, and the power of sacrifice began to eclipse the power of the Vedic gods. This period witnessed the ascendency of the Brahmins to the top of the caste system.

The rigidity and the complexity of the caste system is often attributed to the growing influence of the Brahmins during this period. The original caste system was based on occupation and allowed social mobility. Thus one could change caste by changing occupation. As the self-appointed guardian of the Vedas, the Brahmins closed this loophole by decreeing that one has to be born into a Brahmin family to qualify as a Brahmin

---

[59] In Sanskrit *dvija* means twice born and refers to those members of the caste who have undergone the *upanayana* (thread) ceremony. This initiation ritual is marked by investing a sacred thread that is worn over the left shoulder and across the right hip. The ceremony marks the beginning of sacred duties for Brahmins and the use of weapons for Kshatriyas. For Vaishyas the occasion marks the beginning of their trade apprenticeship. Since the initiation is considered a second birth, people who participate in this ceremony are often called twice born, meaning "having been born a second time from the womb of the guru." The Shudras were excluded from this initiation and were ineligible to study or even listen to the Vedas. Today the sacred thread ceremony still exists but is mostly reserved for Brahmin boys.

[60] Note the differences in the terms *Brahmanas, Brahman,* and *Brahmin. Brahmanas* refers to the ritual compendium of the Vedas. *Brahmin* is the name of the upper caste in the religious hierarchy. A member of the Brahmin caste is also called a Brahmin, although some older texts use the term *Brahman.* The word *Brahman* in Hinduism usually refers to the all-pervading ultimate reality. And Brahma is the creator god.

and then must perform the priestly function. Although not all Brahmins were priests, the Brahmins came up with more rules to preserve their exclusivity, including one that held that each Brahmin had an obligation to maintain the purity of the caste as a whole. Furthermore, contact with lower castes was strictly regulated. Brahmins distanced themselves from the lower castes by defining the functions and duties of those other castes. As masters of ritual and sacrifice, Brahmins claimed the right to respect and to alms.

In those times smaller kingdoms were being swallowed by bigger ones according to what is known as *matsya nyaya,* or "the law of fishes," where the bigger fishes prey on smaller ones. Brahmins increasingly roped in ambitious Kshatriya warriors and created new, expensive, and impressive sacrifices, accompanied by elaborate and more exacting rituals. Soon a Brahmin-Kshatriya alliance emerged with the Brahmins stoking the ambitions of royals who wanted to extend their power. Three new sacrifices were introduced that were not prevalent at the time of the Rigveda. These were the Rajasuya (a royal consecration that ended with the raising of a white umbrella over the monarch's head), Vajapeya (a soma sacrifice that consecrates the ruler as king of kings), and the Ashvamedha (a horse sacrifice in which a consecrated horse accompanied by a troop of soldiers went from territory to territory. If the horse was challenged, a trial of strength ensued. If the horse was not challenged, the ruler was deemed a vassal).

The development of the Upanishads engendered the first reaction to the rigidity of the caste system. Although the Brahmins were very influential in the Vedic social hierarchy, there were opposition to their large-scale animal sacrifices and to their pretensions to superiority by virtue of their birth. The opposition came not only from members of other castes but also from a few Brahmins who chose to ignore the rigid rituals and the caste system. And these Brahmins became the precursors of the creators of Upanishads. The doctrine of transmigration, which introduces the concept of karma and reincarnation, was developed during the period of the Upanishads, as this concept does not appear in the Rigveda.

About 500 BCE, asceticism became widespread and increasing numbers of young men joined the ranks of ascetics in search of the elusive *moksha,* or release from transmigration. The Brahmins reacted to the interest in asceticism by devising the doctrine of the four *ashramas,* which divides the life of the twice-born Hindu into four stages: the *brahmachari* (celibate religious student); the *grihastha* (married householder); the *vanaprastha* (forest dweller); and the *sannyasin* (wandering ascetic). The attempt to keep asceticism in check by confining it to men in late middle age was only partly successful because the Upanishads questioned the divine status of the Vedas and the elaborate ritualism of the Brahmin priests. Instead of declaring the Upanishads works of blasphemy, the Brahmins made the savvy move of incorporating the teachings of the Upanishads into the priestly tradition and the teachings became the fourth Veda. Many traditions that sprang up during this time also questioned blood sacrifice and the killing of animals. They promoted asceticism and vegetarianism, but within a few centuries these ideas also became part of Hinduism. And Hindu mythologies picked up all these elements and modified them through the years.

Religious life underwent significant changes between 600 and 400 BCE. It was marked by the rise of splinter sects of ascetics, who rejected the authority of the Vedas, and supreme leaders who claimed to have discovered the secret of obtaining release from the endless cycle of reincarnation. The important religious figures in these groups were Siddharta Gautama, who later came to be known as the Buddha, and Mahavira Vardhamana, the founder of Jainism.

30

330 Million Gods, Right?

> *India has two million gods, and worships them all. In religion*
> *all other countries are paupers; India is the only millionaire.*
>
> —MARK TWAIN, 1835-1910

By now you may have realized that the concept of god in Hinduism does not have a standard definition. It is not defined by a certain appearance or bounded by a name or confined to a place or restricted by gender. The vastness of the idea of a god—which includes a variety of forms, many places of worship, and multitudes of images, icons, and symbols—has led to a widespread but unfounded belief that Hinduism has 330 million gods.[61] Is 330 million the final tally after taking into account all the gods required to oversee the various portfolios of their vast realm?

The answer is not simple. The Rigveda refers to only thirty-three gods, even though it mentions more than thirty-three by name. The Persians, the historical counterparts of the Vedic people and whose sacred book is

---

[61] Sometimes the number of gods is said to be 330,000,003.

the Avesta, also considered the number of their gods to be thirty-three. The Vedas, however, have neatly categorized the gods: eleven in the heavens, eleven in the atmosphere, and eleven on earth. Other Vedic texts also mention thirty-three gods, which some scholars have interpreted as eight Vasus (attendants of Indra and later Vishnu), eleven Rudras (deities of storm), twelve Adityas (deities of light), and Dyaus (sky god) and Prithvi (Mother Earth). In some interpretations Dyaus is replaced by Indra and Prithvi by Prajapati. In others Dyaus and Prithvi are replaced by the twin Ashvins.

Of the thirty-three gods of the Rigveda, the majority are male deities; it mentions only a few goddesses, who include Ushas (dawn) and her sister, Ratri (night). So where does the figure of 330 million come from? The scriptures mention thirty-three *koti devas*. The word *koti* in Sanskrit means either type or crore (the number ten million). It appears the latter meaning was ascribed to the word *koti*, although an alternative translation would have led to thirty-three types of *devas*. This mistranslation of *koti* to crore probably explains the origin of the 330 million gods in Hinduism. Many Hindus, however, believe that the supreme deity is the one and only Brahman, but they acknowledge it has many names and manifestations.

In this context it is important to remember that the number thirty-three is only a symbolic expression of a particular aspect of the pantheon. In theory the number of gods has no limit, for each manifestation is a channel through which a devotee can reach the divine. The 330 million gods are just a symbolic representation of the many manifestations that were possible.

By the way, how Mark Twain came up with two million gods is beyond me, but I get his drift.

❖ ❖ ❖

31

Prajapati – The Lord of Creatures

At the peak of his powers Prajapati was the greatest deity of the Vedas and more powerful than Indra, Varuna, Agni, or Surya. Like many Vedic gods, however, he gradually lost his standing. When Prajapati is invoked these days, he is often remembered as a creator deity, although not all aspects of his creation are seen in a positive light. Prajapati's greatest claim to fame is the unique sacrifice mentioned in the Purusha Sukta—which is the tenth mandala (10.90)[62] of the Rigveda and dedicated to the Purusha, the Cosmic Being.

The Purusha Sukta, or the "Great Sacrifice of Creation," is a hymn of only sixteen verses written in the older form of Sanskrit. It speaks of Purusha as a cosmic being—a primeval man of mammoth proportions, with a thousand heads, eyes, and feet, and pervading everything. The Purusha Sukta celebrates the sacrifice of this god-like entity, who makes an offering of the cosmic man to himself on a funeral pyre to bring forth all of creation. The whole universe was believed to have been created from the body of the sacrificed Purusha. Thus from his mind came the moon;

---

[62] The ninetieth hymn of the tenth book of the Rigveda.

from his many eyes the sun; from the navel the atmosphere; from his innumerable heads the sky, and from his feet the earth. Purusha is also said to have created the gods—Indra and Agni from his mouth and Vayu from his breath. The *varnas,* or the four great castes of Hindu society, sprang from his body: the Brahmins (priests/scholars) originated from his mouth, the Kshatriyas (warriors) were born of his arms, Vaishyas (traders) sprang from his thighs, and the Shudras (servants) came from his feet.

While the Rigveda dedicates the creation of the universe to the all-powerful cosmic man, the Yajurveda, the Vedic text that came a few hundred years later identifies this single supreme power, which reveals itself in many forms as Prajapati, the Lord of Creatures, in the following lines:

Agni is That, Vayu Is That, Chandramas is That, Light is That, Brahman is That, Waters are Those, Prajapati is He!

In essence, the Purusha Sukta relates a creation myth, and to be fair Hinduism has more than a dozen creation myths. Yet the Purusha Sukta survived to this day even with its modifications and redactions. It is one of the few hymns in the Rigveda that still finds a place today in Vedic rituals and the worship of deities. A modification of this myth appears as Hiranyagarbha, or "the Golden Egg." In this golden egg version of creation, the universe was all waters at the beginning, and the Supreme Being wanted to divide the waters. In the division appeared a golden egg, and this egg produced the first man, Prajapati, who created gods in the sky with light, and *asuras* (demons) in the earth with darkness, thereby creating day and night. His breath brought about air, a woman, a cow, and a mare. He created the power of procreation into his self and divided himself into two people, one male and one female. She became a cow and he became a bull, and they produced calves. This story goes on and on until the whole earth was populated with animals.

Prajapati achieved the height of his glory during the Vedic period, but his powers subsequently waned. In the Upanishads Brahman becomes the ultimate reality, and Prajapati is subordinated to Brahman. By the end of the Vedic period, as Hinduism concentrated on intuitive spirituality instead of the ritualistic sacrifices of the Vedas, Prajapati's significance steadily eroded. Brahma absorbed much of Prajapati's portfolio of functions, such as his relationship with the golden egg of creation. Eventually Brahma supplanted Prajapati in supremacy and was soon seen creating Prajapati as his agent of creation. This single Prajapati morphed into multiple Prajapatis, as later myths describe the creation of a number of Prajapatis for carrying out all aspects of creation. As Vishnu and Shiva grew in power, Brahma became their agent for creation. Brahma in turn subcontracted his job to several—first seven, then ten, and finally twenty-one—Prajapatis, with Brahma identifying himself as one of the Prajapatis.

In Sanskrit *Prajapati* means "lord of the people." In contemporary Hinduism, however, Prajapati has become the name of a group that presides over procreation and protection of life. Nonetheless Prajapati left an indelible mark on Hinduism through Purusha Sukta. The idea of sacrifice, which later became a recurring theme in the Vedas, can be found in these verses. More important, the Purusha Sukta establishes that the Supreme Being creates us out of itself. This has significant implications for Hinduism. While Western religious traditions believe that God creates people out of nothing, in Hinduism people are literally one with the divine and with each other.

Prajapati (along with Brahma and Manu) bears the stigma of creating the caste system, a consequence of Purusha Sukta. The caste system, as everyone knows, had tremendous influence on Hindu society because of its divine sanction. It later became a persistent and pernicious element of Indian society.

❁ ❁ ❁

32

Ekalavya – Caste Is More Important Than Skill

The Nigerian novelist Chimamanda Ngozi Adichie says this about racism in her award-winning book *Americanah*:

The only reason you say that race was not an issue is because you wish it was not. We all wish it was not. But it's a lie. I came from a country where race was not an issue; I did not think of myself as black and I only became black when I came to America. When you are black in America and you fall in love with a white person, race doesn't matter when you're alone together because it's just you and your love. But the minute you step outside, race matters. But we don't talk about it. We don't even tell our white partners the small things that piss us off and the things we wish they understood *better, because we're worried they will say we're overreacting, or we're being too sensitive. And we don't want them to say, look how far we've come, just forty years ago it would have been illegal for us to even be a couple blah blah blah, because you know what we're thinking when they say that? We're thinking why the f?%$ should it ever have been illegal anyway? But we don't say any of this stuff. We let it pile up inside our heads and when we come to nice liberal dinners like this, we say that race doesn't matter because that's what we're supposed to say, to keep our nice liberal friends comfortable. It's true. I speak from experience.*

Racism may be absent in India, but racial inequality in the United States has its parallel in caste inequality in India, even though by definition, *race* and *caste* are not the same thing. Like racism, casteism—the ideological structure based on belief in the superiority of some people because of their birth and the inferiority of others because of the same— is widespread in India, despite attempts by several governments to put an end to the pernicious practice. The creation of Hindu groups of lower castes was, in the words of Mahatma Gandhi, "the hate-fullest expression of caste." Almost one-fifth of India's population belongs to the lowest-caste group, called the untouchables, and suffered centuries of oppression. Nothing illustrates the oppressiveness of the caste system better than the story of Ekalavya, as described in the Hindu epic Mahabharata.[63]

The son of a tribal chief, Ekalavya wanted to learn archery and approached the great guru Drona, who usually mentored kings and princes. A Brahmin himself, Drona refused to accept Ekalavya as his pupil because he belonged to a lower caste. Drona was the archery coach of the Pandava and Kaurava princes (the Kshatriya cousins in Mahabharata who eventually fought against themselves), and his star pupil was Arjuna. Undeterred, Ekalavya made a clay image of Drona, called it his guru, and

---

[63] The Mahabharata is discussed at length in book 4 of this series.

practiced archery day and night, showing the devotion normally reserved for one's teacher, or guru. In due course the intense practice made him a great but unproved archer.

One day the Pandavas went hunting with their dog. The animal wandered off and came upon Ekalavya and stood before him barking. Ekalavya shot seven arrows at the dog's mouth and sealed it shut. What was remarkable was that he had managed to silence the canine with such skill that the animal was barely injured. The dog went whimpering back to the Pandavas, who were astounded by the act and wanted to know the identity of the marksman who had accomplished this feat. They learned it was Ekalavya and that he was an uninitiated student of Drona.

After they reached home that night, Arjuna asked Drona to explain how Ekalavya became a better archer than him, for Drona had always claimed that Arjuna was the best archer. But Drona was perplexed and did not have an answer. To find out the truth, Drona and Arjuna went to see Ekalavya. At their meeting Ekalavya, in all humility, attributed his success to his conviction that Drona was his guru. "If you are truly my pupil, then it is your duty to pay me *guru-dakshina*," urged Drona, referring to the token payment made to a guru for rendering his services. A delighted Ekalavya replied, "Command me, my guru. There is nothing I will not do for you." To which Drona replied, "Give me your right thumb." Ekalavya was horrified at this request, because he would never be able to draw his bowstring again. He nevertheless kept his word and complied.

Later, when the cousins asked their guru to explain his cruelty, Drona replied, "If everybody learns archery, then the tribals will replace Kshatriyas and the entire caste system will collapse, leading to social anarchy. Furthermore, I have promised Arjuna that none of my students would be better than he at archery. To keep this promise I had to stop Ekalavya."

The Valmiki Ramayana,[64] which tells the story of Rama, further corroborates the rigidity and oppressiveness of the caste structure existing

---

[64] The Ramayana is discussed in book 3 of this series.

at that time. To defend the social order Rama slayed a low-caste Shudra called Shambuka because he was practicing penances, which was a violation of his dharma because such privilege was reserved for the upper castes. Furthermore, the epic describes a scene in which Rama had molten lead poured into the ears of another Shudra, who had been found listening to the Vedas.

These myths highlight how sacrosanct the caste system was held in those times, according to which one must follow one's own dharma as defined by the caste. A rigid interpretation of Brahmanism,[65] as stipulated in the Dharmashastras, led to the belief that a person's role in life was already determined at birth. This was not the only time Drona played the role of enforcer of the caste hierarchy. Drona also rejected Karna, another hero of the Mahabharata, as his tutor because Karna was the foster son of a charioteer. Like Ekalavya, Karna never gave up his ambition. He pretended to be a Brahmin and took archery lessons from Parashurama, Drona's tutor, and became one of the finest archers, equal to Arjuna.

As for Ekalavya, he was never the same archer again. In modern India, however, he became a symbol of protest for the Dalit movement,[66] which professed the cruel behavior of Drona as symbolic of the suffering of *dalits* under the caste system. According to them, Drona not only showed his caste prejudice in his treatment of Ekalavya but proved to be the quintessential hypocrite. As a Brahmin, Drona should have been concentrating on his priestly duties; instead he adopted the vocation of a warrior by teaching archery.

---

[65] Brahmanism is Hinduism as defined by the upper castes.

[66] The Dalit movement of the 19th and 20th centuries began in response to the unrelenting hatred and centuries of oppression visited on the Shudras by the upper castes. *Dalit* refers to members of the lowest caste.

> *Caste is about dividing people up in ways that preclude every form of solidarity, because even in the lowest castes, there are divisions and sub-castes, and everyone's co-opted into the business of this hierarchical, silo-ized society.*
>
> —ARUNDHATI ROY, 1961-

✦ ✦ ✦

33

The Caste System of India

When the local government in 2011 provided free midday meals to schools in India's most populous state of Uttar Pradesh, teachers and students refused to participate in the program because the meals were cooked by *dalits,* a group that belonged to the lowest caste in the social hierarchy. But this was not the first time. In fact reactions to social programs like free meals have consistently shown that India's 3000-year-old caste system remains more or less entrenched in the society despite efforts by successive governments to eradicate it. What exactly is the caste system and why is it a blight to society? Let's start at the very beginning.

The division of society into a hierarchy of classes was not unique to India or to the Hindus. But what is unusual about the Hindu system is its persistence to stay rooted in the society through many centuries. The genesis of the caste system can be seen in the verses of the Purusha Sukta of the Rigveda, which speaks of a unique sacrifice that led to the creation of the whole world, including the social order:

> *The Brahmin was from his mouth,*
> *Of his arms was made the warrior,*

His thighs became the vaisya,
Of his feet the sudra was born.

Vedic society was divided into classes, often referred to as *varnas*. The four classes, Brahmins, Kshatriyas, Vaishyas, and Sudras, were said to have emerged from the mouth, arms, thighs, and feet of Purusha, the cosmic man. Originally the divisions were by occupation since the Brahmins belonged to the priestly class; the Kshatriyas, the warrior class; the Vaishyas, the merchant class; and the Sudras, the servant class. Because Purusha's mouth was above his arms, thighs, and feet, the Brahmins were considered superior to the other three *varnas*. The notion that this four-*varna* classification with the Brahmins at the top was cosmically ordained was further asserted in subsequent texts authored by Brahmin priests themselves.

The word *varna*[67] in Sanskrit literally means color, which would suggest four different shades of skin color, each distinctive of a certain class, with the higher classes reserved for those with lighter skin. But this was never the case in India because so many in the upper *varnas* have dark skin and some of the Sudras do not. Originally it was an open class system that allowed individuals to change their *varna* by switching profession. With the publication of the sage Manu's Dharmashastra, the fourfold division of society became inflexible and one's birth determined one's class. According to Manu, the only way to alter one's class was by rebirth, depending on one's accrued karma, a concept that gained currency during the Upanishadic times. New doctrines imposed on Brahmins included the need to avoid contact with lower *varnas* and to maintain the purity of their class. In response to these doctrines the Brahmins did not eat, drink, or perform any ritual without bathing first. They flaunted their superiority by renouncing the consumption of meat and embracing vegetarianism.

Manu also believed that the inter-mixing of *varnas* utterly jeopardized society, an ideology that became central to Hitler's Nazi Party.

---

[67] The term *varna* has many meanings, including color, category, and so on.

However, Manu made some concessions by allowing higher *varna* men to marry lower *varna* women under certain conditions, even though the reverse—lower *varna* men marrying higher *varna* women—was strictly forbidden. Eventually the unapproved mixing of *varnas* led to the creation of many *jatis*[68] (sub-castes) with their own names and occupations. Mahatma Gandhi, for instance, belonged to the Bania *jati* of the Vaishya class. Although the members of *jatis* were supposed to marry only among themselves and maintain the rigidity of the *varnas*, inter-*jati* alliances led to the creation of even more *jatis* and so on. Today most Indian languages use the term *jati*, not *varna*, for the system of hereditary social structures. The original class system slowly evolved into a full-fledged caste system.

The word *caste* originated from the Portuguese word *casta*, which means breed, race, or strain. When interacting with Hindu and Muslim merchants of India, the Portuguese traders of the 16th century used *casta* to label people according to the proportions of Portuguese and other blood in their veins. In the early 17th century, the French in India—and later the British—modified the Portuguese term to *caste* and applied it to the many *jatis* in India. At about this time the caste system was becoming complicated and out of control. Beyond the four major classes were the so-called untouchables, sometimes referred to as outcastes. These were people who did not belong to any caste and undertook the menial tasks that polluted the individual, such as sewer cleaning, street sweeping and butchery. In the caste hierarchy Brahmins were considered the embodiment of purity, whereas the untouchables were the most polluted. Physical contact between the two groups was forbidden. Brahmins adhered so strongly to this rule that they felt the need to bathe if even the shadow of an untouchable fell across them. Furthermore, the untouchables were denied entry to the country's temples. In 1931 Gandhi and

---

[68] Strictly speaking castes are *jatis*, but there's some confusion in usage. Today people loosely refer to the four *varnas* (classes) as the four castes. The *jatis*, in this case, are called sub-castes. The modern word *caste* can refer to *varna* or *jati*.

other reformers pointed out that nearly one-fifth of India's population of untouchables was being systematically discriminated against because of Hindu caste restrictions.

Gandhi looked upon untouchability as a contemptible and abnormal outgrowth of the Hindu social structure. In 1933 he renamed the untouchables *Harijans,* meaning "the people of God." It was proudly accepted by millions of untouchables themselves for their self-identity. After India became independent in 1947, various leaders expressed the hope that India would move toward a classless, casteless society. Subsequently India's Constitution formally recognized the plight of the untouchables by legally establishing their ethnic subgroups as Scheduled Castes. Besides banning untouchability, the constitution also provided these groups with specific educational and vocational privileges besides granting them special representation in the parliament.

Most prominent among the untouchables was B. R. Ambedkar, a noted scholar with degrees from Columbia University and the London School of Economics, and the architect of the Constitution of India. As the leader of the Harijans, Ambedkar gained national attention when he converted to Buddhism in 1956 in a public ceremony. A large number of Harijans followed his lead and converted to Buddhism. Ambedkar died two months later, achieving nirvana in the eyes of his followers. The new converts of about a million came to be called Nav-Buddhas.

By the 1970s Harijans had become a politically active group and adopted the name Dalit, meaning "downtrodden," for their political movement. Yet it took fifty years, from India's independence in 1947 until 1997, for a Dalit, K. R. Narayanan, to become president of India.

Today, even though progress have been made in bridging the caste gap, the traditional divisions between pure and polluted caste groups persist in many levels of Indian society. It is such a powerful force that even non-Hindu communities, such as Christians, Jains, and Sikhs, have absorbed parts of it.

I do not want to be reborn. But if I have to be reborn, I should be born an untouchable, so that I may share their sorrows, sufferings, and the affronts leveled at them, in order that I may endeavor to free myself and them from that miserable condition. I, therefore, prayed that, if I should be born again, I should do so not as a Brahmin, Kshatriya, Vaishya or Shudra, but as an Atishudra.

—MAHATMA GANDHI, 1869-1948

34

Maruts – The Revenge of Diti

An unlucky woman in Hindu mythology is Diti, and that's not because she couldn't beget sons. In fact she and her sister, Aditi, had many children—sons and daughters—and a distinguished sage as husband, for both were married to the sage Kashyapa. Aditi's sons became the Vedic gods, sometimes called the Adityas, who were entrusted with managing the universe and responsible for the activities of the sun, moon, wind, water, rain, and other natural elements. Each Aditya is said to shine during one month of the year and perform his duty. Diti's sons, called

Daityas,[69] became *asuras,* or demons. While the gods were mostly enthusiastic upholders of dharma, the children of Diti were persistent violators, and this often led to clashes with their half-brothers and to the eventual downfall of the Daityas—which became a constant heartache for Diti. As any mother will tell you, no sorrow is greater than the loss of her children.

The ranks of the demons have occasionally produced heroes like Prahlada and Bali, but in warfare they suffered from low caliber warriors who weren't much good at battle. Aditi was giving birth to all the virtuous and powerful gods, while Diti was stuck with sons who were losers. Years of frustration for Diti turned into great bitterness toward Kashyapa and Aditi. Diti cared more about her children's lives than their actions. With the defeat of her famous sons, Hiranyaksha and Hiranyakashipu—slain by Vishnu's Varaha and man-lion avatars[70] respectively—Diti could no longer contain her feelings. She approached her husband, Kashyapa, and said, "You always give preference to Aditi over me. Her children are all powerful, while mine have to flee for their lives. Please grant me a boon that I will have a son who would be greater than the gods. Let my son be the slayer of Indra, the chief of the *devas.*"

Kashyapa was in a quandary. While he had no great affection for Indra, he fancied the sons of Diti even less. Besides Diti and Aditi, Kashyapa had many wives and he loved them equally. He had no reason to grant a special favor to Diti. Yet Kashyapa was sympathetic to her situation. He granted her a boon: she would conceive a son who would exceed the others in prowess but only if she performed the *pumsavana* vow thoroughly. Practiced even today, the *pumsavana* vow is taken to hasten a male fetus, and is observed by women who desire powerful and virtuous offspring. Kashyapa specified that Diti had to maintain absolute piety and purity throughout her pregnancy.

---

[69] Sage Kashyapa had many wives. Strictly speaking the demons include both Daityas and Danavas. While Daityas were the sons of Diti, the Danavas were the sons of Danu, who was also married to Kashyapa. A famous Danava was Vritra, who was killed by Indra.

[70] The ten avatars of Vishnu are the subjects of books 3 and 4 of this series.

Diti soon became pregnant again. But this time she devoted herself with meticulous zeal to fulfilling the conditions of the vow and observed the prescribed rituals for a nearly a century. Meanwhile Indra learned from his tactical device, Indranet, that Diti was carrying a child who would eventually orchestrate his death. So he kept an eye on Diti, ready to strike at the appropriate time. His opportunity came in the ninety-ninth year of the vow when Diti went to bed without washing her hair. With one condition of the vow violated, the boon was rendered powerless. Indra seized the chance and plunged his thunderbolt into Diti's womb severing the unborn child into seven. But the seven parts began to wail so piteously that Indra regretted his action and tried to comfort them by saying, "Ma rodih," meaning "weep not." When they heard his voice, the babies cried even louder. Indra became furious and used his thunderbolt to divide each of them into seven more parts.

The forty-nine beings thus created were called Maruts, from Indra's words of comfort. Far from being Indra's slayers, the Maruts grew up to become fearsome warriors and valuable allies of Indra. With their help Indra later fought Vritra and vanquished the demon. Meanwhile a strange thing happened to Diti. She no longer felt any animosity toward Indra or any of the gods. Committing to the vow for a hundred years had completely purified her heart and dissolved her hostility. Diti felt great happiness and fulfillment when she realized that her husband, who had helped her transform her hostility into love, was indeed a great sage.

In Hindu sacred texts, there is a great deal of doubt about the exact number of Maruts. Although the Ramayana and Puranas state the number to be forty-nine, in the Rigveda they are said to number 180 in some hymns and twenty-seven in others. Many versions of the myth also explain why the Maruts are sometimes called Rudras. After Diti gave birth to the Maruts, Shiva and Parvati held the Maruts in great affection. It is said that Parvati asked Shiva to transform the lumps of flesh into boys. In this sense they became the sons of Rudra (Shiva).

❖ ❖ ❖

35

Changing Roles of Aditi

If Hindu mythology is so confusing that it is driving you crazy, you are in good company. Do you know how many Maruts are described in the scriptures? How about the number of Adityas? Any idea who's the father of Indra? If you are struggling to find answers to these questions, that's okay. The answer depends on which scripture you are referring to. It seems the goalposts are constantly changing in Hindu mythology. A prime example is Aditi, the mother of the Adityas. If you recall, the Adityas are a group of solar deities that includes Indra.

Aditi is one of the many goddesses of Hinduism whose status and roles have changed many times through the years. *Aditi* means eternity or infinite, so Aditi is a personification of time and is mentioned eighty times in the Rigveda. The Rigveda describes her as the mother of Adityas. Originally there were seven Adityas, but that number changed to twelve, and later included all *devas* (demigods). In a later iteration of the Vedas, Aditi became the wife of Daksha, the grandfather of all creatures. During the period of Epics, when the Ramayana and Mahabharata were written, Aditi became the wife of Kashyapa, a progenitor of creation. The Adityas then included all *devas,* so Aditi became of the mother of all gods and goddesses.

Aditi's opposite, in both name and role, was Diti, which means finite or limited. She is mentioned only three times in the Rigveda. Diti's children were the Daityas (born of Diti), who were known as *asuras*. Coming back to Aditi, her status changed further in the Vishnu Purana, in which she became the daughter of Daksha, although she continued as the wife of Kashyapa. In the Devi Bhagavata, Aditi is said to have reincarnated as Devaki, the mother of Krishna.

What explains the changes in roles and status? One reason for these variations is that the gods were born of each other. Another explanation given for variations in parentage or marriage is that these were the results of rebirths—not in this age but in different *manvantaras*[71] with varying roles in each. The concept of *manvantara* is elaborated in detail when we get to Brahma (book 2 of this series).

❖ ❖ ❖

---

[71] Manvantara is an astronomical period of time in Hinduism.

36

Ashvins – Twin Gods of Morning

Celebrated in fifty-six hymns in the Rigveda, the Ashvins are the fourth most popular of the Vedic deities, yet their provenance is shrouded in myth and symbolism. Among the oldest Vedic deities, the Ashvins are a pair of horsemen regarded as harbingers of the dawn. They are, however, more famous for their role as physicians of the gods, and their remedies are mentioned in Ayurvedic medicine.

These twin deities are the children of Surya and Sanjna. Their mythical origin goes back to the time when Sanjna was unable to bear the luminosity of her husband, and surreptitiously retreated to the forest disguised as a mare. After much soul searching, Surya found Sanjna in the forest, turned himself into a stallion, and approached her for companionship. Their courtship resulted in the birth of twins with horse heads. Like their father, the Ashvins are always connected with the celestial light, although their exact nature is not entirely clear. Some interpretations make them day and night, whereas others allude to heaven and earth. Since the Ashvins are considered prehistoric gods, their physical significance probably was lost over time. Yet their association with early morning sun, as morning twilight, is unmistakable.[72] If Ushas represents dawn as the ruddy flush in the east, the Ashvins represent morning twilight as gray light. As harbingers of Ushas, the Ashvins precede the dawn each morning in their golden chariot, which is drawn by horses or birds.

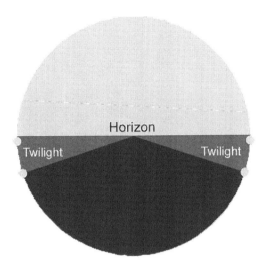

Like Ushas, the Ashvins are both ancient and young, but unlike her they are capable of bestowing youth on men. Although the Ashvins have an illustrious career escorting Ushas daily at dawn, they perform additional roles. As physicians of the gods, the Ashvins are sometimes known as Nasatya and Dasra. It is said that they learned the secret of immortality from Dadhichi, one of the greatest sages of Hinduism. Dadhichi knew the art of Madhu-vidya, which had the power to restore a person from the dead. The lord of the heavens, Indra, felt threatened by Dadhichi's powers and decreed that he would behead Dadhichi if he revealed the

---

[72] Sometimes the Ashvins are said to represent the morning star, one of the nicknames for the planet Venus. Other verses in the Rigveda connect the Ashvins with both morning and evening suns. In this twin appearance they represent the morning and evening stars.

secret of Madhu-vidya to anyone. The Ashvins, as physicians, wanted to add this sought-after skill to their repertoire. They devised a plan to learn the secret from the sage after replacing his head with that of a horse. When Indra learned that Dadhichi had violated his orders, Indra became furious and chopped off Dadhichi's head. But the Ashvins were not perturbed because they had preserved his original head. They restored his head and then revived Dadhichi with the help of Madhu-vidya, which they had learned from him.

Always portrayed as young and handsome, the Ashvins are well known for their benevolence. As physicians of the heavens, they did not limit their healing activities to the corridors of heaven. Rather, they delighted in wandering about the world performing miracle cures on ordinary men and women. Many tales are told about their benevolence, but the most significant is the one involving Chyavana, which got the Ashvins inducted into the ranks of the immortals. Chyavana was an old sage who had been abandoned by his family. Some boys found his decrepit body lying by the wayside and pelted him with stones because they thought he was dead. The sage was enraged by their action and demanded justice. The boys' father managed to appease the sage by offering his daughter, Sukanya, to be the sage's wife.

Meanwhile the Ashvins were traveling about that area performing their cures and met the beautiful Sukanya. One of the Ashvins coveted her, but she resisted his advances, saying she would not abandon her husband so long as she breathed. But the Ashvins were persistent and pursued her a second time. Prompted by her husband, she told the Ashvins that they were anything but perfect. The Ashvins did not understand what she meant but her words piqued their curiosity nonetheless. They struck a deal with Sukanya by promising to restore her husband to youth if she would clarify what she had said. Accordingly, Chyavana bathed in a certain pond and emerged as a young man. As part of the deal, Sukanya told the Ashvins that they were not perfect because they had not been invited to drink soma with the gods at a feast being held in Kurukshetra.

The Ashvins immediately proceeded to Kurukshetra and sought permission to drink soma. But Indra refused, saying that they had strayed from heaven and were performing cures on ordinary people. On hearing this, Chyavana performed a sacrifice for the Ashvins, but a furious Indra rushed to attack him with a mountain in one hand and his thunderbolt in the other. Chyavana reciprocated in kind. Using his ascetic energy, he created a thousand-toothed monster called Mada. When Mada was about to devour Indra, the lord of the heavens conceded defeat and allowed the Ashvins to participate in the soma-drinking session.

The Ashvins are like the Dioscuri, Castor and Pollux, the sons of Zeus/Jupiter in Greek and Roman mythology. Although the Ashvins were important during the Vedic period, their significance as forerunners of dawn eroded over the years. However, they are still extolled for their healing powers, particularly in Ayurvedic medicine. The Ashvins are said to have formulated the popular Indian tonic called Chywanaprash,[73] India's alternative to Western cod liver oil. They also play a cameo role in the Mahabharata, as the co-parents of the Pandava brothers Nakula and Sahadeva.

❋ ❋ ❋

---

[73] Chywanaprash is an herbal concoction of twenty to forty Ayurvedic ingredients and has a jam-like consistency.

37

The Golden Age of Indian Women

If India occasionally reminds you of arranged marriages and their inflexibility, not many people realize that India is also the country that gave birth to *swayamvara*, an ancient practice similar to the popular TV program called Bachelorette. In a typical *swayamvara* the parents of the young woman announce the occasion of marriage by setting the date and venue, and prospective grooms assemble at the scene that day. After scouring the list of suitors, the young woman picks the man of her choice and puts a garland of flowers around his neck, thereby completing the wedding.

Sometimes prospective grooms have to demonstrate their prowess by performing special feats as stipulated by the rules of the competition. Hindu mythology is replete with instances of *swayamvara*, each with its own unique challenges and plots, and the famous ones include the alliances of Shiva-Sati, Nala-Damayanti, Arjuna-Draupadi, and Rama-Sita. For Sita's *swayamvara* the challenge was to lift a heavy bow and string it. Among the suitors only Rama was strong enough to accomplish this feat.

Over time alliances through *swayamvara* became rare, and today it has become just a historical curiosity. Even though it may have faded into oblivion, *swayamvara* reminds us of the high status enjoyed by women in the past in a country where atrocities against women like rape, bride burning, and acid attacks continue to dominate daily headlines.

Rama lifting the bow during the swayamvara of Sita,
painting by Raja Ravi Varma (1848–1906)

In the Vedic age, women were valued and afforded high status. They held roles that were on equal footing with men's, for some of the Vedic hymns appear to have been written by women poets with names like Ghosa, Apala, and Lopamudra. Women were allowed to study the Vedic lore and sponsor sacrifices. Like men, women had the privilege of performing the *upanayana*, or thread ceremony. The ceremony, usually carried out at the age of eight, consists of wearing a sacred thread across the shoulders from right to left and signifies spiritual rebirth—which Hindus call *dvija*, or twice born. In the Vedic age *swayamvaras* were common and child marriages unknown. Monogamy was the rule, and polygamy was frowned upon. The Rigveda contained a few references to the life of a widow, but it was not characterized by the restrictions and austerities that became widespread in the post-Vedic age. Hinduism permitted widows to remarry, and in some cases a brother of the deceased could marry the widow, a practice known as *niyoga*. The Rigveda never mention the gruesome practice of sati[74] in which the widow was burned alive on her deceased husband's funeral pyre.

With the coming of the epics and the Dharmashastras (Hindu law books), the high status of women in the Vedic era began to change. The progressive decline of the position of women in society can be traced through the epics. The early texts of Mahabharata had references to the freedom enjoyed by women when they chose their husbands through *swayamvara*. However, the later portion of the Mahabharata says that Manu instructed women to be under the protection of men because women were deemed physically and mentally weak. Women no longer performed the *upanayana* ceremony. They were prohibited from studying the sacred texts or sponsoring sacrifices. Notions of personal purity had ruled them out for a religious role during the days of menstruation or time after pregnancy. Gradually her intelligence was devalued and equated with that of the Sudras, who were intentionally left illiterate and regarded as incapable of differentiating right from wrong. Male children were given

---

[74] Book 6 describes the disturbing practice of sati.

preference over female, a practice that still persists in the society.

As time passed, girls were considered a burden to the family and married early. The Sutras (short commentaries) have numerous references to marriages of prepubescent girls or infant girls with grooms much older. The Ramayana states that Rama was only sixteen when he married six-year-old Sita. During Manu's time polygamy became so widespread that he tried to limit its incidence by introducing *varna*-based quotas. Thus Brahmins were allowed to have four wives; Kshatriyas, three; Vaishyas, two; and Sudras, one.

As the situation of women deteriorated over time, the double standards within the society, especially gender inequality, started to become glaringly apparent. In this context it must be mentioned that most societies are riddled with contradictions, although these inequalities are more characteristic of some societies than others. One such contradiction widespread in Hindu society lies in the worship of the mother goddess. From time immemorial Hinduism had celebrated the concept of a mother goddess that personified the dynamic forces, or Shakti of the primordial cosmic energy. A number of scholars, however, have highlighted the apparent paradox in the treatment of female divinities and everyday women. The contradiction gained notoriety after the publication of Mrinal Pande's 1983 short story entitled "Girls," which is told from an eight-year-old's perspective and highlights how Indian society takes women for granted and prepares them to accept a secondary role in the family. The rebellious daughter in the story confronts her mother with such questions as "When you don't love girls, why do you pretend to worship them? If female power empowers the universe, how is it that women are often belittled in their everyday actions?"

Other contradictions existed in post-Vedic society. Men could openly keep any number of mistresses, but women were punished for infidelity. There are rituals like *Vatasavitri* in which women propitiated to god asking for the same husband in the next birth. No corresponding observance exists for men asking for the same spouse in his next birth.

Sociologists who have studied the position of women in ancient India have acknowledged that the gender landscape is complex because of paradoxical statements in scriptures. As a result, their conclusions often end upon on the opposite sides of the gender spectrum. While some have described women's overall status as equal to men, others have characterized it as disrespectful or downright outrageous. It appears that women enjoyed the status of Devi (goddess) only in theory, but were subservient to men in practice.

However, some Hindu attitudes toward women were consistent at all times. Hinduism has always deified mothers and held them in high regard. Each partner has an equal role in the performance of marriage vows. Most Hindu rituals are performed in the presence of both husband and wife. And every year Hindus celebrate the platonic relationship of women and men—whether young, old, related by blood, or otherwise—with a bonding festival known as Rakshabandan.

It appears that while society's regard for women remained more or less the same, the rights of women changed over time. From a position of complete equality in the times of the Vedas (1500 BCE–500 BCE), women lost status by the time of Manu (200 CE). For that reason the Vedic period is often referred to as the golden age of Indian women.

❖ ❖ ❖

38

End of the Vedic Era – Vedic Pageantry

If it wasn't clear by now, Vedic society consisted of simple pastoral people organized around nature gods and living in the northern regions of ancient India. Their fondness for inspirational poetry, however, was unprecedented in the history of Hinduism. When lightning struck in the Vedic age, it was orchestrated by Indra or Vritra or Rudra, depending on the effects. Drinking and attacking someone was not Dutch courage, rather the unmistakable trait of Indra. Skirts flying skyward and wardrobe malfunctions were not merely unfortunate accidents but engineered by the wind god Vayu. If you thought the breaking of Internet by the Kardashians was just a modern-day deviance, then the ancient *apsaras* were routinely breaking the resolutions of revered rishis, gods, and demons with their own unique brand of overt displays.

Beneath the bravado of the heavens, the central theme of the Vedas was to seek identity with nature and adapt one's way of life around calamities like fire, flood, drought, famine, or earthquakes. The core message of the Vedas was one of assisting humans to conduct their journey of life toward a meaningful and purposeful end. With anthropomorphic external forms, the Vedic gods were identified with the forces of nature. The role of human beings was to acknowledge the power of the deities and to please them with sacrifices through offerings centered on fire which served as a bridge between humanity and divinity. These may have been the factors that have helped the Vedas to prosper in India to this day, because the natural environment has remained the same for many thousands of years, with people dependent on the forces of nature—mountains and rivers, the sun and the stars, monsoons and seasonal changes—for their prosperity.

If the Vedic gods and goddesses are lined up for pageantry in the liking of a Miss/Mr. Universe contest, who do you think would win? In the preceding chapters, we have explored the deities and mythology surrounding them. We have examined, cross-examined, and even re-examined the characters and witnesses in excruciating detail. Having watched the swimsuit and evening gown categories and followed them up with the talent rounds and the personality tests, we are now in a position to announce the winner. And the winner of this Vedic pageant is unquestionably Indra, the lord of the heavens. Although not a single temple is dedicated to him today, more than one-fourth of the Rigvedic hymns were dedicated to Indra alone, underscoring his popularity during this period. The table that follows lists the popularity of the deities according to the number of hymns dedicated to them in the Vedas.

Position	Deity	#Hymns in Rigveda
Winner	Indra	289
1st Runner-Up	Agni	218
2nd Runner-Up	Soma	123
3rd Runner-Up	Ashvins	56
4th Runner-Up	Varuna	46

Indeed, the heavenly spectacle was more like a Mr. Universe contest. The only goddess of any significant merit during the Vedic period was

Ushas, the goddess of dawn. Although the gods Indra, Agni, and Varuna were popular in this period, a notable omission was Surya, the sun god, even though his twin sons, the Ashvins, found a place in the top rankings. The Ashvins were physicians of the heavens, and people often ask, "Why do gods need physicians?" At this point, we should not lose sight of the fact that the Vedic deities are *devas*, or demigods, and considered inferior to the Trimurti (triad) of Hinduism comprising Brahma, Vishnu, and Shiva, the *mahadevas*, or great gods. Later mythology explains how Krishna put Indra firmly in his place as a secondary deity.

By the end of the Vedic period, the power and stature of the Vedic gods had diminished. Their children, however, assumed significant roles in later mythology. Arjuna, the protagonist in the epic Mahabharata, was the son of Indra. Surya's son Karna also plays a memorable role in the epic. Although the Vedic gods were replaced by other gods in later mythology, they continue to hold a special place among Europeans scholars of the 19th and 20th centuries, who were fascinated by the child-like, pure, and innocent virtues portrayed in the myths of Vedic India. These scholars believed the Vedic Aryans were the closest intellectual relatives of the Europeans. One keen admirer of Indian mythology was the German poet, philosopher, and Indologist Friedrich Schlegel, who considered the Rigveda the mother of all mythology. For Max Müller, the German scholar of religion and mythology, Vedic Aryans were the cousins of Europeans, and the culture of West came from India. But modern Indians, according to him, had degenerated from the Aryans, for contemporary Hinduism offered only a trace of the Vedic revelation even though the cultural heritage of the original Aryans survived intact in Europe.

Muller's characterization of Vedic India continues to haunt modern academic scholarship even today – and has led to serious political repercussions in race theory.

Index

D

E

F

G

W

Y

Z

About the Author

The view was magnificent and the panorama spectacular. That's me, Sach, perched on a ledge in the Himalayas, the mountain range that stretches across six countries of the subcontinent. Indeed nothing gives me greater joy than standing on top of the world's highest mountain range. It brings a sense of fulfilment, for I've been researching Hindu mythology for the past decade or so. And, trust me, some of these myths are as old as the mountain. In fact mythology speaks of the time when the Himalayas were growing taller and taller—a fact scientifically corroborated—making them the envy of other mountains in the vicinity. The mountains occupy a special place in Hindu mythology, as we'll learn from this series. The Pandavas meet their fate on the mountain. Parvati, the charming wife of Shiva, is said to have been fathered by the Himalayas.

For me, scaling this mountain was a lifelong quest. Although I have achieved it with the help of my friend Photoshop, the real dream lives on.

Made in the USA
Middletown, DE
05 November 2018